STARTING YOUR CAREER

AS A

SOCIAL MEDIA MANAGER

Praise for *Starting Your Career as a Social Media Manager*

"There are lots of authors giving advice to organizations on how to do social media. All of these organizations need qualified professionals to develop and execute their social media strategies. Thankfully, Mark Story offers something different: practical, no-nonsense, experience-based counsel to jobseekers who want to make social media their careers. The world didn't need just another social media book; the world needed this one."

—Christopher Barger, author of *the Social Media Strategist*

"If you want to get hired in the fastest growing sector of marketing and public relations, stop everything and read this book right now." —Eric Schwartzman, coauthor of *Social Marketing to the Business Customer* and founder of SocialMediaBootCamp.com

"Mark Story has delivered a master's degree in launching a career in social media in book form. For an industry that is young and evolving—yet has such awesome potential for you—this is the go-to resource for getting started and understanding what you need to know to be successful. As I turned each page, I thought, *Man, I wish I had this advice when I was in college!* Very little of this is being taught in colleges now. But it will be soon. And this is probably going to be the textbook."

—Jason Falls, CEO of Social Media Explorer and author of *No Bullshit Social Media: The All-Business, No-Hype Guide To Social Media Marketing*.

"Mark Story provides grounded advice on how to achieve a meaningful, results-oriented career in social media. Avoid mediocre results in your social media job and frustration with the marketing organization by implementing the great advice in these pages."

—Geoff Livingston, Author and Marketing Strategist

"From SEO experts and communications professionals to direct marketers and advertisers, everyone has jumped onto the social media bandwagon claiming to be an expert. But the true pros are those who are up for constant challenges, aren't afraid of change, are willing to take risks, and are willing to hone their craft every single day. It's time to take advantage of the opportunities in our industry and Mark Story is just the person to teach you how to do it."

—Gini Dietrich, CEO, Arment Dietrich and coauthor, *Marketing in the Round*

"Whether you're a student just getting ready to start your career or a professional seeking to make a change, you need a path to follow. Mark Story has charted the course for you in *Starting Your Career as a Social Media Manager*.

"If you want to go places in your career, follow Mark's map. He is the first-ever director of new media at the United States Securities and Exchange Commission. Think Sarbanes-Oxley and all the precarious situations social media may offer your employer. Mark has dealt with them.

"Mark gets it. He does not serve up Kool Aid. We are grateful that Mark has spoken to many classes at Auburn University. The students are always thankful for his guidance and advice."

—Robert French, professor, Auburn University

"My public relations students often say to me, 'It's gotta be FUN working in social media!' I think it's high time for them to read Mark Story's new book to learn that working in social media is real work. He breaks down careers in social media and what it takes to prepare for them in a clear and easy-to-read way. This book is a must-read for all PR students; it's going on my required list now."

—Barbara B. Nixon, PhD (ABD), assistant professor of public relations, Southeastern University

STARTING YOUR CAREER

AS A

SOCIAL MEDIA MANAGER

MARK STORY

ALLWORTH PRESS
NEW YORK

Copyright © 2012 by Mark Story

All rights reserved. Copyright under Berne Copyright Convention,
Universal Copyright Convention, and Pan American Copyright
Convention. No part of this book may be reproduced, stored in a
retrieval system, or transmitted in any form, or by any means, electronic,
mechanical, photocopying, recording or otherwise, without the express
written consent of the publisher, except in the case of brief excerpts in
critical reviews or articles. All inquiries should be addressed to Allworth
Press, 307 West 36th Street, 11th Floor, New York, NY 10018.

Allworth Press books may be purchased in bulk at special discounts for
sales promotion, corporate gifts, fund-raising, or educational purposes.
Special editions can also be created to specifications. For details, contact
the Special Sales Department, Allworth Press, 307 West 36th Street,
11th Floor, New York, NY 10018 or info@skyhorsepublishing.com.

15 14 13 12 11   5 4 3 2 1

Published by Allworth Press, an imprint of Skyhorse Publishing, Inc.
307 West 36th Street, 11th Floor, New York, NY 10018.

Allworth Press® is a registered trademark of Skyhorse Publishing,
Inc.®, a Delaware corporation.

www.allworth.com

Cover design by Brian Peterson

Library of Congress Cataloging-in-Publication Data is available on
file.

ISBN: 978-1-58115-925-7

Printed in the United States of America

CONTENTS

FOREWORD

Whether you have bought this book, have been assigned to read it as part of a class, or are simply thumbing through it at a bookstore, you might be asking yourself this question: "Is a *career* in social media for me?" I emphasize the word "career" because there are precious few opportunities to select a professional path that involve such constant change and challenges, and that require honing your craft on an ongoing basis. Many people whom I know come from other professions such as broadcasting, marketing, communications, public relations, or public affairs, and grow into the role of a social media practitioner, but I know very few people who have left the field.

Throughout the book, I attempt to impart my experience working as a practitioner in the field, being a professor at the graduate-school university level teaching online communications, and also as an author, podcaster, and general social media addict—all towards the goal of helping you meet *your career goals*.

The advice that I offer in this book is based on my own experience, but over the years, I have had the absolute joy of befriending and learning from some very smart people, many of whom have offered here their insights into how you can start your own career in social media. These experts' thoughts and opinions show up throughout the book, but since you may be getting started and thinking "How can I do this?", it's worth taking a look at how many of the leading minds in the field started their careers. You may be surprised.

Meet the Experts: How They Got Started in Social Media

In the chapters that follow, you will get some solid, "been there, done that" advice from social media practitioners who have attained a high level of job satisfaction and achieved success at many different levels in the profession. The thing that most people won't tell you is that there is no secret sauce to success—and no secret to preparing for success. Many practitioners are self-taught and come from diverse backgrounds. Here is a sampling of how some of the people in this book got started in their careers in social media:

- *David Almacy, former Internet and e-communications director at the White House.* David graduated from Widener University in Pennsylvania with a degree in business management with a focus on marketing. "While I was in college, I interned for then-Vice President Dan Quayle, between my junior and senior year in 1991. They offered me a permanent job, asking me if I would jump out of school and work at the White House. The Gulf War had just ended and President H. W. Bush's ratings were in the 90s. 'What could happen?' My parents told me to stay in school, so I stayed. And some governor from Arkansas won the election."

- *Christopher Barger, senior vice president of global programs for PN Connect and former head of social media for IBM and General Motors.* "My undergraduate degree is in history at the University of Minnesota and my first career was political campaigns. I worked locally in Minnesota and in Washington, DC as well. Then I went to Boston University for graduate school. I got to be the Dean's T.A. and specialized in corporate communications. I got into social media very much by accident. I had worked at IBM for six years, and I settled in as a speechwriter. I was going to write novels when I graduated. It was the spring of 2003 and blogs started popping up. My boss rode me for three months, telling me that 'you should do this.' Finally, I gave. Over the course of the next year, I started blogging, and in about a year and a half, I had built up about 5,000 unique visitors a week. In February of 2005, I got called down to the head of communications for IBM, and that in and of itself was daunting, because junior speechwriters do not get called to headquarters. He said, 'I've been reading your blog for about the last six months.' I thought,

'I'm dead. He's gonna fire me.' He said, 'There is going to be a business application for this blogging thing, and I know that you know how to build a community. I want you to figure out how this is going to work for businesses and how this can benefit IBM.' So I went from getting fired to getting promoted in about twenty seconds. And I really focused on blogging. If I hadn't listened to my boss in the spring of 2003, my career would be a very different story."

• *Brian Carter, author and consultant.* "I was a profit-oriented skeptic with a background in search engine optimization and pay-per-click advertising. 'I have too much of a life for Twitter,' I told my agency CEO, before it took over my life in 2008. 'Facebook marketing can't possibly work,' I said in 2010, before getting dragged into Facebook marketing by a client. But then I resolved to master it. I learned in part by reading blog posts, but more by experimenting and speaking privately with others who were being creative and running tests to discover what worked best. Facebook Marketing 101 and FanReach were courses I taught to six thousand people before writing *The Like Economy*."

• *Chuck DeFeo, head of digital media at the American Center for Law and Justice and e-campaign manager at Bush/Cheney '04.* "I was never a programmer or a technologist, but I was a suburban kid with a computer. When I moved to DC in 1996, I worked for a United States senator who was forward thinking in technology, and he had an issue that he wanted to bring to the floor in the form of an online petition. The only problem was that there was no one in the office who knew HTML and could do a web page. I was an intern and had not even been in the office eight weeks. I had never really, actually created a web page. I crammed for a couple of days and I launched the first online petition by a member of Congress. That was in March 1996. It was only up for two weeks, and we had 70,000 people sign it. In 1996. This made the front page of *USA Today*, the *Los Angeles Times*, and the *New*

York Times, generating significant national coverage—and I was some intern! I was hired a couple of weeks afterwards."

- *Robert French, professor, Auburn University.* "After I graduated from Auburn, I was offered two jobs. One was writing for the *Huntsville Times* and one was to work for the Easter Seals Camp ASCCA (Alabama's Special Camp for Children and Adults: http://www.campascca.org/). They had never done any publicity. Computers were just starting to be used and I began doing mail merges. Spray and pray. In one summer, we'd get 15,000–20,000 column inches in state newspapers—because we personalized every story for every county. We sent along glossy photos when we actually developed pictures in a darkroom."

- *Antonia Harler, social media strategist, Paratus Communications, London England.* "I am self-taught. My education is in management and IT. I did a semester in the United States at the City College of New York and my undergraduate degree at the Management Center Innsbruck, Austria. I took a PR course and it frightened me. There was no one to teach me about social media, so the only way I had to learn it was by buying books like the *Social Media Bible* and others and teaching myself. But you are only going to learn it by doing it."

- *Dr. Julia Hill, PhD, professor and director, public relations program, Graduate School, University of Maryland University College.* "I came to academia after twenty years at a city administration and a police department. It was through the evolution of my life as a public relations practitioner when I was involved in the first-ever developmental website for my employer. We were always looking for ways to connect with people, to find the strategies and tactics to help develop long-term relationships with constituents, with the people whom you serve."

- *Evan Kraus, executive vice president and director, APCO Online.* "I studied aerospace engineering at the University of Virginia. I thought I was going to build rocket ships. When the industry experienced a downturn, I parlayed knowledge about satellites into a job at Booz Allen. While there, I became interested in all things technical and realized that he had a passion for customer service. I joined APCO in 1996 because our owner realized that the Internet was going to impact our business."

- *Geoff Livingston, author and marketing consultant.* "I was a horrific student at American University, a literature major. All I had was this writing skill. The only job that I could get was based on an internship I had at the Electronic Industries Association. I started doing public affairs work and writing stories about technologies like Mosaic, which is viewed as the first web browser and precursor to Netscape. And these weird people like Tim Berners-Lee (recognized inventor of the World Wide Web) and Marc Andreessen (inventor of Mosaic). We were communicators, but we were all geeks too. I worked at a dot-bomb in California and then got into the agency side of the business. During the recession, they turned me onto sales and I was really good at it."

- *Kristen D. Wesley, agency social media consultant.* "My interest in social media began in graduate school at Georgetown University. I became inspired by a class called the Intersection of Online and Offline. I realized that social media was something I could sink my teeth into; it was traditional, yet it was new and at the forefront. While at grad school, I created a path for myself that was 'all social': every course that I took had to have a component of social media in it or I created a project for the class that dealt with social media. I graduated two years later and I started looking around for a social media position (I was working full time at the time, but not in social media). I didn't know if I wanted to work for an agency or an association. I was not sure what I wanted to do. I got a call from my current employer and they told me that they received my resume from a friend who was in the graduate program at Georgetown as well. They had a position available for digital. I went through a grueling process and proved to them that I had lots of experience in social media, even though I was not a full-time practitioner. And I got the job, as a Team of One.

Social Media and *You*

If you noticed anything about the preceding list that almost everyone has in common, it is that they set out doing *something besides social media*, and stumbled into the profession. If there are patterns within the list, they are that, educationally, our "experts" prepared themselves through writing and/or information technology. Both are at the heart of social media.

All of these social media practitioners started out in different stages in their lives with different aspirations—and have become successful.

You can, too. Let's get started now.

CHAPTER 1

MAKING THE CHOICE FOR A CAREER IN SOCIAL MEDIA

Peter Gibbons: "Our high school guidance counselor used to ask
us what you'd do if you had a million dollars and you didn't have
to work. And invariably what you'd say was supposed to be your
career. So, if you wanted to fix old cars then you're supposed to be
an auto mechanic."
Samir: "So what did you say?"
Peter Gibbons: "I never had an answer. I guess that's why I'm working
at Initech."

— Scene from the 1999 classic cult movie *Office Space*[i]

Peter Gibbons and a Career in Social Media

Office Space is one of my favorite movies of all time. At the crux of the
movie is the protagonist, Peter Gibbons (played by Ron Livingston),
and how much he hates his job at his employer, Initech. He is so
miserable at work that, among other coping mechanisms, he seeks
out the help of a hypnotist to help make him numb at work. He and
his friends try to cope with their misery. They sneak out of the office
on long coffee breaks, make fun of coworkers, smash copy machines,
and end up stealing thousands of dollars (inadvertently) from Initech.
And they are still miserable.

This scenario has played out for me as well as my friends and
colleagues; *Office Space* has been not a movie, but reality. I have
been miserable because I have made poor choices, and I bet you
have, too.

This book is the "Initech repellent": it's a guide to help you make
the right choices if you are interested in a career in social media. It's

about gathering enough information to make a good choice, having the intellectual curiosity to investigate the field, and putting in the work to become successful. And any book that begins with a Peter Gibbons quote *has* to good, right?

The Importance of Making the Right Career Choice

Career happiness can mean more *life* happiness. Consider that when you choose a job, at a minimum, you can expect to spend anywhere from eight to ten hours per day commuting to and from work, carrying out your job responsibilities, or just thinking about them. Most people spend eight hours sleeping, so that leaves you less than eight hours a day and weekends and vacations for other pursuits. The bottom line is that you will be a whole lot happier if you choose a job and career that you enjoy. You're investing a lot of time into a career. Choosing a place where you will happy spending the majority of your waking hours can greatly improve your quality of life.

Is a Career in Social Media for You?

The Jobs Are There
New social media tools and platforms have created a demand for practitioners who get it—and can make the best use of strategies, tools, and tactics to help organizations achieve their communications objectives. Consider the following statistics on how social media has exploded over the last several years. All of these points will impact either your job choices or how employers will view you[ii]:

- *User base is growing.* Eighty-six percent of people aged 18–29 use social networking sites. This is up from 83 percent in December 2009 and 67 percent in May 2008. Younger people are current or future professional social media practitioners. And let's say that your potential boss falls in the 50–64 age bracket. Her use of social networking sites has grown from 11 percent in May 2008 to 47 percent in May 2010. So both potential hiring managers and employees are adopting social networking sites at an astounding pace.

- *Your potential employers are creating jobs for you to fill.* Seventy-one percent of companies use Facebook, 59 percent use Twitter, 50 percent use blogs, 33 percent use YouTube, 33 percent use message boards, and 6 percent use MySpace (which has fallen off the social media radar). And an anticipated 43 percent of companies will employ a corporate blog in 2012. Employers who are adopting these tools will need people not only to help them implement them, but to use them to achieve communications or marketing objectives.

- *Facebook rules the roost.* If Facebook were a country, it would be the world's third most populous, with 900 million people.[iii] Seventy-five percent of brand "Likes" come from Facebook advertisements. The fastest-growing segment of Facebook users is college-age people (a great statistic if you are thinking about starting a career in social media right out of college).

- *Twitter is growing —sort of.* While Twitter has nearly 200 million users and the total number of daily tweets grew 252 percent from 2010 to 2011 (27 million in 2010 to 95 million in 2011), 49 percent of users rarely or never check Twitter.[iv] This is one of those examples of "all that glitters is not gold." While the statistics indicate that the total number of users and tweets is growing, if an entire 49 percent of users rarely or never check their accounts, it's like shouting in an empty room. This tells me that many people use Twitter—a lot—but an almost equal number set up accounts that languish.

- *Your online resume is LinkedIn.* Widely recognized as the "online resume" of social networking tools, the total number of LinkedIn users has grown from 50 million in 2010 to 119 million in 2011. And it's not just people looking for jobs; 95 percent of companies who use social media for recruitment are using LinkedIn in 2011.

- *Don't forget about email.* Eight *trillion* emails were sent in 2009.[v] Email marketing is still an important tool in the social media practitioner's toolkit.

- *Mobile/smartphones continue to grow in popularity.*[vi] According to February 2012 statistics gathered by the Pew Internet & American Life Project, 87 percent of American adults currently have a cell phone; as of May 2011, among cell phone owners, 42 percent own a smartphone, and 87 percent of smartphone owners use their phones to access the Internet or email, with 78 percent of these users saying that they go online using their phone on a typical day. Age is the primary differentiator—a full 94 percent of smartphone owners ages 18–29 use their phones to go online, with eight of ten (81 percent) doing so on a typical day. The explosion of how people use their phones, the information that they choose to receive, and how you can get your organization's message to them all bode well for the future of mobile communications.

- *These same potential employers are doing research on you.* While many people have adopted social media to build an online profile, not all of the information is viewed positively by potential employers. Fifty-three percent of employers reported researching potential job candidates on social networks, and

  o over a third said that viewing a social networking profile proved that candidates had lied about or misrepresented their skills on a resume;

  o 13 percent said that a potential employee had made discriminatory comments on their Facebook page; and

  o 9 percent of potential employers found provocative or "inappropriate" photographs posted on a Facebook profile.

Need More Convincing?

SimplyHired.com, a job aggregator website, noted at the end of 2011 that, based on search terms that appear within job listings on their site:

- LinkedIn jobs increased 456 percent;
- Facebook jobs increased 30 percent;
- "social networking" jobs increased 18 percent; and
- MySpace jobs decreased 34 percent.[vii]

Potential employers are recognizing that social media should be an intrinsic part of their communications efforts, and this will continue to create a demand for skilled practitioners.

What You Need to Consider Before Starting Down the Social Media Career Path

Whether you are graduating from college or considering a career change in order to be successful in social media, you'll need to engage with a lot of people, both internal and external clients, and try to make them happy.

Your Career: Working with Internal Clients

Your professional path can take you many places, but most will have you working with two types of clients: internal and external. For the purposes of this book, internal clients are your coworkers—perhaps in a large corporation, a government agency, an association, or a non-profit. You might be doing blogger relations, monitoring customer sentiment, or building and maintaining external platforms like Facebook or Twitter, but on behalf of one client: your employer and other internal stakeholders. Working "in-house" has its own set of opportunities and challenges, but when you are thinking about a career in social media, you will need to know:

- Why does your employer want to use social media? What are they trying to accomplish?

- Will you have the resources, both in fiscal and human capital, to achieve what your employer wants to achieve?

- Can you get top-level support if and when internal turf wars break out over social media? We'll talk about this later in the book, but social media has many perceived masters, those who want to and think they "own" it: marketing, public relations, public affairs, government relations, and IT, as well as legal.

- Do you have the ability to manage internal politics, managing up and down the corporate food chain?

Your Career: Working with External Clients

Working for external clients usually means that you are working either for a digital agency or working within the digital practice group of a larger public relations or public affairs firm. While many of the job requirements and tasks are the same, whether you are working in-house for a firm or serving clients for an agency, there are some important differences, especially when you are evaluating career alternatives. The main difference working for an agency is that you need to juggle more than one client, pay close attention to budgets and billable hours, and balance the needs of the clients while trying to also respect your colleagues' time and efforts. When considering a career in social media on the agency side, you will need to think through the following questions:

- Are you willing to work long hours and balance the needs of multiple clients simultaneously?

- How do you define success for your clients? What communications objectives do your clients want to achieve and how they will be measured?

- How do you manage your clients' understanding of social media, tolerance for risk, or interest in using new tools?

- What budget is available to do what they are asking you to do? (We used to say that many clients had "champagne taste and beer budgets.")

- If—and only if—online is right for them, how can you help them select the right platforms to achieve their communications objectives?

- How can you marry their expectations with what is reasonable?

- Can you effectively manage timelines and budgets?

- Can you measure your efforts based upon what you set out to do?

Your Career Working in an Agency: Juggling

If you choose a career in social media within an agency, you will have an additional group of people to make happy: internal constituencies. The graphic designers might not like the fact that the client does not like their design, the programmers might not like the expectations that the client has, and the project managers may well be going crazy trying to hold everything together.

When I was at Fleishman-Hillard, I was head of the project management team in Washington, DC, the largest digital practice in the Fleishman global network, meaning that I managed a group of twelve people who, we used to say, had the hardest jobs at the agency. We had to work with web writers, programmers, graphic designers, usability experts, internal client contacts, agency management, and others, and do so in an environment of shifting client needs, expectations, and demands. We often had to go back to our colleagues internally (mainly the writers, graphic designers, and programmers) and tell them that their hard work needed to be redone based on a client's changing needs or whims. And many times, I had promised my internal colleagues (after receiving assurances from clients) that a version of something was the *final final*, only to have to go back to them on a Friday afternoon at four-thirty and tell them that I needed them to work over the weekend. Those are unpleasant conversations, but not wholly uncommon in the agency world.

Is It for You?

A career in social media can be rewarding, intellectually stimulating, challenging, and financially lucrative—but there are also many, many challenges if you work for internal or external clients. The bottom line is that happy internal and external clients usually make for a happy career.

When a Career in Social Media Might Not Be for You

Kristen D. Wesley, an agency social media consultant, told me that a career in social media might not be for you if "you are not interested in learning new things on a daily basis. You really have to be OK with not knowing everything and learning quickly. A lot of people like to be the expert in everything right away. [And then] one day Pinterest shows up, and if you are not willing to try to learn it, feeling stupid for about five minutes and then moving forward, a career in social media is not for you."

Don't be Peter Gibbons. Know when to spot a bad match. Not every career is for everyone; it's a good idea to think about when a career in social media is *not* right for you. Based on my experience in working in the field, as well as working with others, here are some red flags that should warn you to stay out of the field.

- *You prefer to work alone.* While there are social media consultants and even some full-time staff who work alone, for the most part they have earned that right through honing their craft as part of a larger team. Building a career in social media means that you will have constant interactions with other people. They might be marketing people, communications staff, IT folks, or lawyers. Building and maintaining a successful social media program is based upon "social work"— meaning collaborating, negotiating, and working well with others—and being professionally "sociable." If you strongly prefer to work alone, this may not be the field for you.

- *You hate change.* In the world of social media, the only constant is change. Almost monthly, new technologies, platforms, widgets, and perspectives appear that have the potential to impact the efforts of your organization or your client. Who knew that Facebook would grow to have more than 900 million users (and growing), while MySpace would become largely irrelevant? Or that Twitter would help individuals, citizen journalists, and professional journalists break news stories? In the online world, tools, strategies, and tactics change *all the time.* So, in order to establish yourself and remain successful, you have to readily adapt and embrace change.

- *You are not a fan of consuming media.* Note that I did not say "you are not an avid reader," because staying up-to-date on changes in social media is about more than just reading newspapers or books. To be successful and adapt to changing environments as I have noted above, it is not only important but *critical* to stay current with what is new and noteworthy in the world of social media. This information might come from influential blogs, from online news sources like Mashable, from someone's Twitter feed or Facebook page, or even from YouTube. And yes, books too (hopefully, like this one!). I'll go over this more in the pages that follow, but good social media practitioners are voracious consumers of information. If you don't like consuming media, I would not pursue a career in this field.

- *You can't stand to be frustrated.* Many careers carry with them a fair amount of ingrained frustration. But as I noted earlier, working in social media can generate a fair amount of frustration and stress. You will need to teach people about social media who are afraid of "losing control of the message," when it has already happened. You'll need to fight turf wars with other people, many of whom are less qualified, who want to "own" your social media properties. You will likely have to deal with legal or compliance processes to make sure that your messages or those of your clients are legally vetted. Moreover, you will also have to keep your colleagues on the same page, and you could have a whole team of user experience architects, usability experts, graphic designers, programmers, blogger relations, writers who specialize in the web, and project managers—of all whom need to hit the same deadline that your boss or your client expects. There are many inherently challenging or frustrating components to a career in social media, so consider these carefully.

- *You hate writing.* Above all other skills sets, being a good writer is at the top of the list for being successful in social media. "Social" is about communication, collaboration, cooperation, and being part of groups—and a great deal of this collaboration is via the written word. Sure, using Facebook, Twitter, or communicating via texts constitutes social media, but earning a living in the field means that at many points in your career, you will have to convince internal or external stakeholders via the written word. If you work in-house somewhere, you will likely have to write a memo or talking points about why you want to try a new technology on behalf of someone else.

If you work at an agency, writing skills are even more critical. The profitability of an agency depends upon the ability of its employees to grow new business and expand existing business. You will do that using the written word via client updates, explanations of major projects, and proposals. I'll present a lot more information on the importance of writing in the next chapter, "Preparing Yourself for a Career in Social Media."

My Path to a Career in Social Media

I did not really choose a career in social media; it chose me. This is common for people my age who enter the social media field. I was born in 1964 in New Hampshire in a house with one black-and-white television set, one channel (PBS), and until my late twenties, no exposure—at all—to anything remotely related to the online world. The first time I ever saw a computer was while attending the University of Maryland in the early 1980s.

My first-ever job in Washington, DC was as a cold-caller for a temporary agency. I earned a whopping $14,000 a year during my first year: not exactly Rockefeller money. It was tough and required a tolerance for constant negotiation and rejection—but then again, it made me resilient. I have often told myself that if I can walk the streets of Washington, DC in August toting a bunch of brochures in my hands and knocking on doors for almost certain rejection, then I can do almost anything. This has helped prepare me mentally for many of the challenges that I have faced since then. Preparation for what will become *your* career may come in many different forms, be it a Harvard education and a prestigious internship or the night shift at McDonald's.

After working in the employment industry, my career took a turn toward communications. Since I had just finished my master's degree in marketing and was then placing high-tech people (programmers, database administrators, etc.) in jobs, I got hired as the marketing director of a high-tech company in Maryland.

This was my first foray into the Internet (and my own *Office Space* job, but perhaps that will be the subject of another book). Among other things—and this was the mid '90s—the company built websites. As soon as I saw what went into building a website, and how you could actually inform and persuade people, I was hooked. So the combination of marketing study, experience, and an interest in the technical side of things led me to what was really the beginning of a career in social media.

I officially began my career in what was *not* called social media in about 1997. With a background in technology marketing, I was hired by a boutique online public affairs firm in Washington that was then called The Bivings Group, and my job title was "director of online business networks." I had no idea what that meant (and sincerely doubt that my employers did, either), but knew that they were going to pay me to do some Internet stuff. So we made up the job title, made up the job description and the responsibilities, and off we went. We built external websites, intranets (internal websites), extranets (private websites that one can access over an Internet connection with an ID and password), and other shiny gadgets. This was my first taste of Internet evangelism—and the background in sales and marketing helped too. In short, I was hooked.

This job took me to larger employers such as the public affairs firm APCO Worldwide, the global public relations firm Fleishman-Hillard, and now the Securities and Exchange Commission of the United States. At each stop, I have had conventional or unconventional titles: "vice president," "senior vice president," and "director of new media." No matter what my title was, however, I still needed to *figure things out* once I got there.

Social media job titles and responsibilities are like that. It's hard, especially for potential employers, to figure out what they need or what you will be doing, so a lot of what is traditionally concrete in other fields is vague in social media. Despite a detailed job description—or one that is vague—you will likely end up making stuff up on the fly, especially if you want to advance your career (I'll cover this in more detail in chapter 9, "Getting Started: Figuring It Out"). The field of social media always brings something new, so there are few places where one can just slide into a job and be done with it. There is a lot of on-the-job training.

When I landed at each stop working in social media, I asked myself: What was I supposed to do? What did the internal and external clients need? What technology tools were available to me, either in-house, off-the-shelf, or from a third-party vendor? How did I define and measure success? These were the easy questions, though. The harder question dealt with understanding the internal needs, knowledge, and capabilities of your company or agency and of your external clients.

How Others Got Their Social Media Careers Started

At various points in this book, you'll read solid advice from social media practitioners who have achieved various levels of success. Don't be intimidated if you don't have a background in social media if that is your chosen field, because most people don't. Building a successful career in social media is more about preparation in other fields like public relations or writing than it is about having instant success out of school. Consider the first job of some of the folks you met in the foreword of this book. Like my first job as a cold-caller for a temporary agency, almost no one got their start in what we now call social media.

- *David Almacy, former Internet and e-communications director at the White House.* First job: broadcast services division of the Republican National Committee producing "news actualities" at 3:00 a.m.

- *Chuck DeFeo, former e-campaign manager, Bush/Cheney '04.* First job: a converted internship in the office of a former senator from Missouri.

- *Robert French, professor, Auburn University.* First job: doing publicity for Easter Seals Camp ASCA in Alabama.

- *Antonia Harler, social media strategist at Paratus Communications, London England.* First job: paid internship doing IT.

- *Evan Kraus, director of APCO Online.* First job: aerospace engineer consultant, Booz Allen Hamilton.

- *Geoff Livingston, author and marketing strategist.* First job: writing stories about technology based on an internship at the Electronic Industries Association.

Many of the successful practitioners that you'll meet or the leading thinkers in the field did not get a start in social media right out of school, but prepared themselves using many of the strategies and tactics that you'll read in this book. And, as you'll also read, they "figured it out."

Summary

The growth of web-based platforms, and the degree to which they are being adopted, is creating tremendous career opportunities. Just because the opportunity is there, however, does not mean that it is necessarily right for you. Your choice of a career will have profound impact on your life; it can be the difference between wanting to get out of bed in the morning and head off to work—or not (again, think of poor Peter Gibbons in *Office Space*). And if you decide to get out of bed and head off to your job in social media, you will find challenges whether you are working in-house or for an agency, but if you choose the right place to work, you can also reap rewards and career satisfaction.

In the next chapter, we'll cover how to get yourself ready through self-education and scholastic learning, internships, and other methods.

CHAPTER 2

PREPARING YOURSELF FOR A CAREER IN SOCIAL MEDIA

"Let our advance worrying become advance thinking and
planning."
—*Winston Churchill*

Turning "advance worrying" into "thinking and planning" will become your own preparation for a career in social media. It will be what you do to put yourself in a position to succeed, both academically and professionally.

As you saw in the Foreword and in chapter 1, in the past there were few well-defined paths to success in social media. There are new ways available now to help you succeed in social media and learn about tools, tactics, and key skill sets like writing: avenues like college study, internships, and self-teaching.

When it's time to make a decision as important as where you are going to work (and not end up like Peter Gibbons in *Office Space*), you want to make an informed choice. This means doing your own thorough research and investigation, and working with others through talking, listening, and learning from social media professionals.

Preparation through Knowing the Tools

As mentioned in chapter 1, "Making the Choice for a Career in Social Media," there are increasing adoption rates of social networking sites throughout all age groups. This has created a demand for qualified professionals.

What these statistics *don't* show you is that just because you understand the basic and "top five" tools in the world of social media does not mean that you are an expert and can apply your knowledge effectively in a professional environment. For example, if you are on Facebook, do you know how to do more than post status updates, add pictures, put things on friends' walls, and play Farmville? What about setting up groups or establishing organizational pages on Facebook? What if you work for a governmental agency that does not allow advertising on Facebook pages? Finally (and most importantly), how well do you know the ever-changing privacy policies of Facebook, especially given that at the time of writing, they are under heavy federal government scrutiny?[viii] Being familiar with a platform like Facebook is not the same as knowing all of its features, policies, and implications.

The key to making the jump is adequate preparation. We'll start with education.

Advice from David Almacy, former Internet and e-communications director at the White House:

Q: What advice would you give someone who is considering a career in social media?

A: It's the same advice that I would give to a person who is interested in a career outside of social media. If you have an interest in digital, you should be a personal advocate of it. Use the technology."[ix]

Preparation through Classroom Learning

There are precious few academic programs in the United States that offer true and meaningful guidance on how to learn about communication first, and social media second, then how to combine the two to become a good advisor. I am going to offer a few examples of college programs that I think offer good practical training on how to become a successful practitioner. Among them are the Georgetown University School of Continuing Studies (I created and taught a graduate-level course there called The Intersection of

Online and Offline), the University of Maryland University College (I taught there as well), and Auburn University, led by the insightful and highly respected professor Robert French.

My Course at Georgetown: "The Intersection of Online and Offline"

It's rare that one has the opportunity to create a course from scratch and teach it. I did. It was an exhilarating experience to create something from nothing and teach real-world strategies and tactics. We used textbooks that guided our study, but each and every week, I attempted to weave in personal anecdotes based upon my years of professional experience.

In order to be a good social media practitioner, you first need to be a good communicator, and in my course at Georgetown, I began my course by studying the field of public relations and the fundamentals of communication. I did so because social media is message over medium. You can have the latest and shiniest tools out there, but if you do not understand how to craft, convey, and measure the effectiveness of your messages, you will not be successful. An in-depth understanding of communications (broadly defined) and public relations (a bit more narrowly defined) is the first step in honing your craft. Again, to craft and deliver a message using social media, you first need to master the art of message creation and delivery.

I still keep in touch with many of my former Georgetown students and am proud to say that many pursued careers in social media (like Kristen D. Wesley, whom you'll meet in this book). Their own professional journeys have taken them to social media practices within large public relations agencies, as well as roles within associations and other private sector employers. I have heard from them as well that a sound base of understanding communication helps inform an effective social media program. Here are a couple of examples of good programs.

Expert Insight: Interview with Julia Hill, PhD, professor and director, Public Relations Program, Graduate School, University of Maryland University College.[x]

Q: Why did you decide to incorporate social media into the curriculum at UMUC?

A: It was a natural for us to incorporate social media into almost every course that we provide and there are three reasons why. First, our program is aimed at public relations practitioners. We try to develop a curriculum on what is important for them. Second, social media has become an increasingly important tool or tactic in communications programs—their potential employers. Ultimately, it would have been irresponsible of us to *not* make social media part of our program. Third, what we do not offer is courses that are solely about social media. For me, that is the same thing as having a course just on news releases or just on one tactic. What we try to do is say that strategy is first and tactics are second, and what we try to do is to combine the two.

Auburn University

Robert French is one of the pioneers in teaching social media as well as in developing a very hands-on course that teaches undergraduate students how to prepare themselves for a career in social media. Robert is widely respected in both academic and professional circles. He is also the founder and brains behind PROpenMic (www.propenmic.org), an online resource that connects students, faculty, and social media and public relations practitioners, offering biography pages (an online resume of sorts), member-based blogs, discussion forums, video interviews with prominent practitioners, networking events and opportunities for extended learning, job boards, and what I think is most important, a place for people (mainly students) to post their own resumes. It is a groundbreaking, helpful resource if you are thinking about starting a career in social media. If you have gotten this far in the book and are interested in pursuing a career, join PROpenMic now.

Since Robert is not only an educational pioneer but one who has a vision of how to prepare undergraduate students to work in the field of public relations and social media, I interviewed him in December of 2011 to get his take on important issues to consider when mulling over or pursuing a career in social media. The questions and answers follow:

Expert Insight: Interview with Robert French, professor at Auburn University[xi]

Q: How did you get started teaching?

A: My first semester at Auburn [in 1999], they wanted to create a class called Style and Design. Computers were pretty new. I told them that I would set up the course. At that time, I started noticing blogs. I started just writing about what we were doing on Auburn. Back before open source, I bought some software to publish online and made my students write feature stories and releases and publish them online. The software cost $350.00.

I saw [online] as the place where things were going; the low cost, the opportunity for experience and interaction with other people as they were blogging. We never sought attention, but it brought us [Auburn] publicity. That never would have happened except for social media. Our success is the argument for doing social media.

Q: Did your course evolve over time as the platforms changed?

A: Sure. As new platforms emerged, we added them as long as they added value. I tried to keep it down to the basics. We started doing online stuff on AuburnMedia.com, but not all of it was public. Style and Design and Public Relations Messages is a composite course. In the course my students create digital portfolios—like internships and work experience—and it then becomes their personal brand. They have their own domain.

Q: Describe your course, Style and Design and Public Relations Messages.

A: First of all, before we even start, we start trying to get my students talking and thinking about social media and break them of any expectations that this is how they are going to *use* social media for business—and help them understand that it is a different type of relationship building. We primarily focus on Twitter and Facebook and posts on Auburn Family (http://family.auburn.edu/). Every time they write a post for the site, I tell them that they have to promote one of their own or one for a fellow student. It's a reach/frequency type of process. I total up the friends and followers and tell them what sort of a reach they could have.

Q: Is writing important to a career in social media?

A: We are communicators first, and the main way that we do this is through writing, so if you can't do that, let's find another career for you. You are probably not going to do well. Writing is the number one thing. Students get mad because I make them write a lot. Writing on Twitter, writing on Facebook, writing two feature stories online, and producing two videos per week.

Preparation through Self-Teaching

While writing this book, I have heard from many junior- and senior-level practitioners that there are simply not enough institutions of higher learning that offer courses or majors in social media. Most focus on the field of communications—public relations or marketing—and add on social media courses. That's what I did at both Georgetown and the University of Maryland University College.

Antonia Harler, a social media strategist at Paratus Communications in London, told me, "There was no one to teach me about social media, so the only way I had to learn it was by buying books like the *Social Media Bible* and others and teaching myself. But you are only going to learn it by doing it." Antonia's point of view mirrors those of my contemporaries for whom not only were educational opportunities not available, this thing called "social media" did not even exist! Courses of study like those offered at Georgetown, the University of Maryland University College, and Auburn are more the exception than the rule. So if you are interested in a career in social media, be prepared to pick out a set of books, read, teach yourself, and start exploring on your own.

As you prepare yourself through formal classroom education or self-teaching, remember that in social media, the only constant is change. What is hot today may be obsolete tomorrow. Learning about the fundamentals of communication is critical; if you fully understand things like messaging, channels, and measurement, these skills will help you make better decisions when choosing the most effective social media tools.

Evan Kraus of APCO Worldwide makes an even starker point about education vs. constantly studying what's new in social media: "If you studied social media two years ago in academia, you would be wrong today. What works today will be very different than what worked two years ago. If you grew up studying advertising or PR, those skills are relevant, but they are not sufficient. People need to have the intellectual curiosity and the hunger to keep learning and studying what's best."

Preparation through Internships

Sometimes the best way to get your foot in the door in social media—or in any other job field—is to work as an intern. The deal made between an employer and intern is that you will give you them your time and efforts for a greatly reduced salary or for free, and they will teach you about the field that you want to enter.

In every job I have had in the social media agency world, we have not only had internship programs, we have relied on them heavily as a source of cheap labor. In the summertime, we would wait for the crop of interns to come rolling in to help us with grunt work—or even to fill out the company softball team!

To add some perspective, the *Chronicle of Higher Education* sums up the value of internships from the individual's perspective as follows:

> Internships are negotiated partnerships, so it is helpful to consider the cost-benefit analysis from multiple perspectives. Benefits to interns may include academic credit, salaries, benefits, practice in disciplinary skills, material for disciplinary reflection, exposure to the habits of professional practice, increased self-awareness, the opportunity to exercise civic responsibility, expansion of social and professional networks, and résumé building.[xii]

The Benefits of an Internship

When you do an internship, you get job experience, experience in learning either a practice or something as simple as a professional phone manner. Other benefits include:

- *You will get real-life, hands-on job experience that you can't get in an educational environment.* You'll learn everything from how to operate a complex copy machine to how to write for internal and external audiences (there's that writing thing again). If you choose an internship in social media, you will likely learn how to strategically apply what you might know intuitively about platforms like Twitter, Facebook, or SMS (text messaging). If you get the right mentor, you can learn about what to focus on, what to pay attention to, whom within the company you should to try to work with and learn from, and perhaps how to play (or avoid) office politics. A really good internship mentor will also help you make decisions about where you want to go with your own academic or professional career.

- *An internship is like taking a career for a test drive.* In what should be a relatively low-pressure environment, an internship should give you day-to-day exposure to what it's like to work in a field without having to sign on full time. For example, although there are internships and clerking positions available for law school students, I know many, many people who have gone to law school only to find out that, when they started working at a law firm, they hated it. Most stay until the student loans are paid off, but many of my friends have said, "I wish I knew what I was getting myself into." Well, an internship at the right place in the right environment can, in fact, let you take a career for a test drive before you commit as a full-time employee.

- *You are building your resume.* A resume is a presentation of your professional and academic accomplishments. An internship gives you the opportunity to accumulate evidence that you can, in fact, work in your desired field. Especially if you can get a recommendation from a supervisor—and sites like LinkedIn make this easier than ever—you can prove to future potential employers that you have come away from college not only with educational experience but with proof of your abilities to be successful in your chosen field.

- *You can begin to accumulate contacts.* What most people at the intern phase in their lives lack, even more so than experience, are the contacts that can help them gain exposure to job opportunities. You can hopefully either meet the "right people" within the organization where you are doing your internship, or even meet people outside of the firm in other places that are interesting to you.

Internships Can Help You Build Contacts

When I interviewed David Almacy, the former Internet and e-communications director at the White House, I asked him about the importance of making contacts and networking for those who want to start a career in social media. He told me:

> There is nothing that replaces in-person contact, the power of networking. Offer to take people to coffee, offer to take them to lunch. Usually people like to be asked for counsel and advice. Put the seed in their head. Go out, be aggressive, and join social media groups. Social Media Week happens in many cities. It's not hard to find a lunch or happy hour to go and network. Get a business card and follow someone on Twitter. It's about being visible both online and offline. Start a blog and write about something that's happening the social media world and what you think about.[xiii]

Preparation through Mastering the Basics: Sound Communications Fundamentals

While I was interviewing people for this book, I asked all of them about the traits that they thought a good social media practitioner should possess. Not surprisingly, all of the senior people whom I interviewed focused in on one skill set: being a good communicator. Period. Full stop.

You can't be a good social media practitioner without being a good communicator. You will spend much of your career explaining, teaching, convincing, and persuading before you even get to touch the social media tools.

Being a social media person without the sound underpinnings of communications fundamentals is like trying to live in a house built on a shaky foundation. It can stand for a while, but with that first big wind or storm, its weaknesses will be exposed and it will collapse.

Let's begin with writing.

The #1 Preparation Tool: Good Writing

Developing cool Facebook pages or clever tweets will only get you so far. You will need to be an excellent communicator first, and at the heart of communicating is writing, telling a story.

Dr. Julia Hill of the University of Maryland University College told me of writing for the public relations professional:

> It's not just important: it's essential. Public relations, at its base, is a writing profession. I think that what social media has created is a need for more versatile writers. Now you have to be able to write a compelling 140-character tweet, write a compelling blog post, write a YouTube script, or craft a thoughtful response to a stakeholder post on your blog. And this is in addition to all of your other writing that is still important, like newsletter articles, speeches, announcements, etc. So all of this is an add-on to how important it is to be not only a good writer but a versatile writer capable of performing in all sorts of media.[xiv]

To develop and advance a career in social media, you'll need good writing skills to:

• Get your foot in the door with an employer using an *error-free resume* that helps tell your story, along with a compelling cover letter (although I think that cover letters matter much less than resumes). One typo in your resume or a sloppy cover letter sends the message to a potential employer that you either do not take writing seriously or you lack the requisite skills.

• Show off your online writing skills to potential employers through an online medium like a blog. There is a different standard for blogging—it is much less formal than print, but you still need to apply the basic fundamentals of crafting a good story, and gaining and keeping the reader's attention. You need to craft compelling content that will draw readers in and make them want to continue reading. You need to write crisp, concise sentences, have compelling headlines, and link often to information that supports what you are saying.

How Good Writing Will Help You Once You Land the Job

When you get a job in social media, you will put your writing skills to the test in many different ways. You will spend a lot of your time teaching and convincing people with your writing. You'll need to prove that you are smart and that not only are you an expert on social media, but you can also convince people to become interested in or give the green light to projects that you recommend. Good writing is not just for memos, though. In social media, good writing touches many other areas.

Writing for Search Engine Optimization. If your focus is on gaining attention for a website, you need to know how to write well for SEO (search engine optimization). Even when you write for the web, you are still telling a story, but SEO is a specialized skill that involves things like knowing how many times to use a word on a page (keyword density—this helps with Google rankings), which words to use, and how to craft a page that is easy to read. Good SEO writing is important when you try to gain attention for your blog, Facebook page, or perhaps Google+ profile.

You Can't Be Face-to-Face with Everyone. Social media still scares a lot of people, so if you want a successful career in the field, you will need to spend a lot of time explaining topics that are simple to you but complex, scary, or meaningless for others. In the business world, for both internal and external audiences, you likely won't have the opportunity to explain things to someone in person. The fancy term for this is "asynchronous communication," but it just means that the moment in which you send the message is not the moment in which the person receives the message. Think of an email that you send and your boss does not read for a few hours.

If you work in-house doing social media for an organization, you may have a great idea, but often it's difficult to get your boss's attention. Part of successfully "managing up" means that you can't spend time with her whenever you want. You'll need to do a lot of written persuasion.

Agency Work: Proposal Writing. Writing proposals, or at least participating in the process, is a given if you work for an agency. The larger the agency, the more proposals you will likely work on. These proposals are often in the form of a response to an RFP (Request for Proposal) that will spell out (hopefully concisely) what a potential client is looking for. You and your colleagues must then read the proposal carefully, both respond to questions and try to divine the intent of the RFP, and *use the written word to convince your potential clients* that your ideas, staff, and solutions can solve the problems or opportunities that they have put before you.

At every agency where I worked, we did proposals. A lot of them. What was surprising to me was, even in a business in which compelling writing was a must, probably only 25 percent of the people with whom I worked really understood how to write a good proposal response. Many could write effectively, but responding to questions in a persuasive and concise format is critical.

How Proposal Writing Works. Generally, the way that it works is when your agency finds out about a business opportunity, you will ask to be included in the "RFP list"—and you will get the solicitation when the company issues it. In a good agency, there will be a "kick-off meeting" to begin the process, in which those who will participate in the writing process will get together to talk about how they will respond. Again, the larger the agency, the more offerings you will present, including perhaps social media, advertising, public affairs, lobbying, and grassroots capabilities. Good proposal responses usually follow these steps:

1. A "kick-off" meeting is held in which the people who are going to contribute to the process will either do a phone call or have a face-to-face meeting to discuss proposal themes, writing assignments, and timelines (someone involved in the writing process is *always* late and misses a deadline—plan on it). By selecting a theme for the proposal, everyone has an outline or idea of the main points to get across.

2. The writing gets divided up. Within the agency, different people in different departments will have different writing assignments, yet still need to adhere to the main points and themes that have already been decided.

3. The written portions are finished and presented to an internal editor. Being the proposal editor is the worst job in the whole process. Not only does this poor person have to nag everyone who is supposed to be doing client work to meet the writing deadlines, but in order make the proposal writing flow, he also has to take many different writing styles and edit them to make sure that the proposal comes out in a consistent manner, reflecting one theme, one voice, and one approach. Most people (hopefully all) assigned to the proposal will write well, but everyone has a different written voice. Combining all of these into one cohesive document is a thankless but critical job.

4. Graphics are added. Writing is an important part of graphic design. When I worked at Fleishman-Hillard, we had one person whose job was to craft graphics solely for the purposes of business development. It was our job to explain to him what we were trying to say so he could take that story and turn it into a chart, picture, bullet points, or all of the above. When you employ graphic design, you use fewer words, so the words that you use matter even more. Being a good writer means giving good counsel to your graphics person.

Finally, and likely after some internal fights, your proposal response is edited, looks great, and makes it out the door. I have been involved in probably more than a hundred proposal projects, and only once or twice did we turn in the proposal more than a few hours early. Because of the pressure involved in bringing in new business, people argued, nagged, and worried. But everyone is relieved when the process is over.

Some Best Practices for Proposal Responses. As I mentioned, good writing is hard; you need to spend time and effort to make sure that your words convey your meaning in an easy-to-understand manner. Here are some additional tips for proposal response:

1. Subject, verb, object. Write simple sentences that are easy for people to understand, especially when you are writing about social media. Avoid flowery terms, multiple uses of catchall phrases like "engagement," and tell your story in a straightforward and easy-to-understand way. If your potential client wants to increase their market share selling widgets, tell them that you understand what they are trying to accomplish in a concise manner. Provide short, declarative sentences with easy-to-understand concepts that tell them how you will do it.

2. Organize the document well and give it a flow. State your understanding of their issue, then lay out in a logical order how you plan to help. Like this book, use lots of numbered or bulleted lists along with headers and sub-headers. Dense text is much harder to read; well-organized, concise documents are easier on the reader's eyes and have a logical flow. Remember that there is a human being on the other side of the proposal evaluation process who has to read and grade yours and likely others' responses to the proposal. This human has limits as well and could easily be tired of reading when they get to yours. It's also human nature to want to get through reading as soon as possible, so this underscores your need to make your point in a concise manner and move on.

3. Know when to stop. Stop writing when you think that you have effectively conveyed your message. Extraneous words in a proposal can actually annoy a potential client rather than persuade her. I have always believed that less is more. We used to call it the "thump test." If, when printed and bound, the proposal makes a "thump" noise when you drop it on a table, you should go back and edit it down to a more manageable amount of words.

4. Use graphics only when they help. When I was at Fleishman-Hillard, they were in love with charts and graphics—and they sure looked good. But many times I had the sense that we included graphics simply to have them. Visual elements in a document need to help explain your point—and have a point for being included. Don't throw in charts and the dreaded infographic unless they truly add to the persuasive elements of the document. And if you *do* add an infographic, remember that the first part of "infographic" is *information*. Make sure that your picture easily conveys the information you want it to.

5. Use bios only when they are requested. Both at APCO and at Fleishman, we would often include bios of the people who were perhaps going to work on an account if we won the work. The bios were standard and canned, and sometimes had nothing to do with actually proving to the client that that individual could add value to the account. And for God's sake, don't include pictures. On the client side, when I have issued and had to read volumes of proposals, I don't care what your team looks like. I don't care if they are handsome, fat, ugly, or have three heads. I just want to know that they can help me and my organization achieve what we have set out to do.

6. Price ultimately matters most. You can craft the best-written document in the world, but often, a client's decision will come down to price. You can have all of the wonderful writing in the world and visuals that nail your points, but if your price is considerably more than the company with an inferior proposal, you

might not get the work. But you still need to give it your best shot, which means writing well with the intention to inform and persuade.

The Importance of Good Writing for Internal Audiences. While responding to proposals when you work for an agency is one of the hardest challenges for writers, when you work in social media *within* an organization, you will likely have to have good, persuasive writing skills as well. This is true at almost all levels.

If you are junior and the first and only person to hold a social media role within an organization, soon after being hired, you will likely need to put together a written plan of what you plan to accomplish and what you need to get the job done. Just as with responding to RFPs in agencies, you will need to craft documents that inform and persuade your colleagues. The informing part is easier, but to truly persuade one or more people within your organization, you need to think carefully about how your approach meets the needs of your employer and *why it makes sense.*

Too many times, internal discussions involve a frustrated social media person who says "BUT WE HAVE TO BE ON TWITTER!"—and who gets blank stares. Instead of getting frustrated, take your time, craft a document that focuses on what your employer's communications plan attempts to accomplish, and spell out how using Twitter will help achieve those objectives. Again, be concise and persuasive. Subject, verb, object. Then circulate the document to those who have the power within your organization to approve your plan (paying close attention to the chain of command).

Writing for PowerPoint. For many, "writing" and "PowerPoint" do not belong in the same sentence. Heck, there is even a popular book denouncing PowerPoint as a way to convey ideas: *Real Leaders Don't Do PowerPoint: How to Sell Yourself and Your Ideas.*[xv] For me, writing for PowerPoint is a necessary skill. Not everyone likes PowerPoint (or Keynote, for the Mac lovers), but almost everyone uses it to present ideas, inform, and persuade. Don't think for a minute, however, that using PowerPoint as a persuasion tool means abandoning good writing skills. In many cases, it can make good writing skills even more important.

In the case of a written document, you have plenty of white space on a piece of paper to persuade someone. In some ways, that's easier, because you can organize your ideas and give flesh to your main points. When you use PowerPoint, and especially when explaining or selling social media, you need to be a good enough writer to distill complex ideas into easy-to-understand and meaningful words—you just don't have enough space for anything else. Being a good writer also means being a good editor, so your challenge is to organize your main ideas and reduce them to bullet points or very short sentences—in a way that someone who is not there when you present it in person can understand. Many use PowerPoint as a crutch when making presentations, but it's still necessary.

When I worked for Fleishman-Hillard, we often used a different approach. We developed storyboards (big, foam-backed posters using graphics that conveyed our ideas) and eschewed PowerPoint presentations. While this put an onus upon us to really know what we wanted to say and persuade verbally, I liked this tactic. Think about the people in the room when you offer up your PowerPoint. Half of the time, they are looking up at the screen where your slides are projected: this means that they are only half paying attention to what you are saying. When you use a storyboard, your audience can only read it so many times. At some point, they will turn their *full attention* to you.

Summary

Like a football coach studying an opponent before a big game, preparation is everything. Learning the fundamentals in an academic environment can be difficult because there are not many undergraduate and graduate schools that teach the foundations and practice of social media. This leaves you with the choice of applying to one of the programs listed here (and perhaps moving), or choosing the path of teaching yourself.

In chapter 3, "Applying Your Experience," we will cover the next steps. Now that you have considered a career in social media, learned about it, and thought about how to prepare yourself to work in the field, it's time to strike out and begin to look for your first job.

CHAPTER 3
APPLYING YOUR EXPERIENCE

"Experience is simply the name we give our mistakes."
—*Oscar Wilde*

Even younger people who don't have a lot of formal social media training are often surprised when I tell them that they have more experience than they think. And once you gain that experience, even if it's through self-teaching and building your own tools, is valuable.

At some point along your path to becoming a professional in social media, you'll begin to say, "OK. I'm ready." Then it's time to begin building your online portfolio, or as some call it, your "personal brand." This is like hanging a billboard out and saying: "I'm great. I get it. Hire me."

Creating the Portfolio That Will Help You Get Hired

"You've heard the horror stories: a job applicant gets turned down because his potential employer discovered his objectionable tweets, or saw pictures of his keg party on Facebook. There is a lot of advice out there about keeping your online activity from hurting your career. But there's a flip side. When handled correctly, social media can help you professionally. You can use it to enhance your personal brand, establish yourself as an expert in a field, or demonstrate fluency with all things digital. The key is to be proactive about managing your activity and image."

More than ever (and almost always in the social media field), potential employers will look you up online. Period. Full stop. If your desired job is in social media, you can guarantee it. Rather than leaving it up to others to define you online, make sure that you play an active role in shaping your online profile—build the platforms you want employers to see and promote them.

Step #1: Check for "Digital Dirt"

If you are active in social media already, before you can begin building your online profile, you need to check what already exists online with your name attached to it. In short, you need to act like a potential employer and research yourself. Here are a couple of steps:

1. Sign out of Facebook and Google your name and any other identifying information. By logging out of Facebook, you'll get to see what potential employers will see because they have not friended you.

2. Click through the results—carefully. You may have done a good job by locking down your Facebook profile, but what about your friends? Have they tagged you in posts or pictures that are publicly accessible? Are these the sorts of things that are acceptable to you if a potential employer were to find them?

3. Also look for tweets, blog mentions, and anything else with your name attached to it. If you have a profanity-laced tirade against an old boyfriend in a blog post that you forgot about, you probably want to remove the post, if not the whole blog. If you are mentioned by friends in a way that you think compromises a professional online profile, like a tweet: ("Me and @mstory123 got SO WASTED at work last night!!!"), you should ask your friend to take it down.

4. In short, do the online research, housekeeping, and cleaning up before your potential employers start looking you up.

Step #2: Use Existing Services to Build Your Online Profile

Samples of online tools that will help you build this searchable body of work include a solid LinkedIn profile, an insightful blog (it doesn't have to be genius, it just needs to express what you think, preferably about social media), and a fairly frequently updated Twitter account as well as a public-facing and open profile on Facebook. As I write this, the jury is still out on Google+, but it is growing exponentially in popularity. It may well need to be part of your promotional arsenal as well. These are all elements that can portray you in a positive light and, if you have interesting things to share and what you blog about is fairly well-written (read: error-free), that will help you look informed and smart.

As you learn about, evaluate, select, and begin to really build your online portfolio, here are some suggested sites that can help show employers that you "walk the social media walk."

LinkedIn

LinkedIn is by far the closest thing to an online resume, and its reach is enormous. On March 22, 2012, LinkedIn announced that its membership had exceeded 100 million members—a huge community. [xvii]

A good LinkedIn profile contains many of the elements that could and should comprise your accomplishments as presented in a resume. It even has a tool that ranks the completeness of your profile and encourages you to continue building it until you reach what they think is your best offering—and they call this "100%." Here are some tips about putting your best foot forward on LinkedIn—and feel free to benchmark my suggestions against my own LinkedIn profile, www.linkedin.com/in/markstory!

- *Have a good profile picture, not one that is cropped of you at a party.* If you don't have one, dress up and have a friend take a picture of you. Look professional.

- *Consider expanding the network of people with whom you are connected.* But have the people in your network make sense. If there is a hiring manager who is "two degrees" separated from you, it makes sense to send them a LinkedIn invitation. Someone who plays in a garage band in Portland, Oregon, might not make sense to be in your network. Consider one additional thing (and this is something that bugs me): if you are taking the time and effort to search for someone, consider their value as a contact, and when reaching out to them, *please* customize the LinkedIn connection request. The current LinkedIn default message is "I'd like to add you to my professional network on LinkedIn. —Mark Story." If you want to add this person and connect with them in a meaningful way, take thirty seconds to customize the message.

- *Get recommendations.* For some people, reaching out to others for professional recommendations on LinkedIn is awkward. I think that reaching out to people for networking purposes, online or in person, is essential: this mirrors how the interview process works. You send in a list of your educational and professional accomplishments (a resume), and if and when a potential employer is interested, he/she will contact your references. LinkedIn makes this easy. It's a couple of clicks to ask someone to recommend your work, but again, customize the request. If you know the person well enough to ask him or her to recommend you, send a note first of all asking, and second, explaining the reason for the request. And be prepared to reciprocate. There is a built-in function in LinkedIn that enables you to, in turn, recommend the person "back." It's also a good idea to gather at least one recommendation for each employer or educational stop.

- *Plug in other social media accounts.* On my LinkedIn account, I have plugged in my Twitter feed (@mstory123) and my tweets are displayed on the home page of my LinkedIn profile. My tweets or re-tweets give insight as to what I am interested in, what I think, who I think is worth re-tweeting, and generally what is important to me. It easy to do and when done correctly, also gives visitors to the page more insight about you.

- *Join a LinkedIn group.* There are thousands of groups on LinkedIn; consider them to be crowds of people with whom you can interact to further your own professional goals, and who share common interests with you. For example, the "Washington, DC Connections" group has more than 29,000 members who presumably, in a city that values connections, want to *connect.* More importantly, there is a DC-based group called "DC Recruiters" [xviii] whose sole purpose is to exchange information about job openings. There are recruiters and job seekers in this group. Why not join and be exposed to new people and new opportunities? The group's organizer recently posted a terrific infographic, tracking the group's growth from 2007 to 2011. The group currently boasts more than 3,700 members, all of whom presumably share the same interests: hiring someone or being hired.

- *Spend time writing the summaries of the accomplishments or descriptions of each job you have had.* Craft them carefully and using words that put you in the best possible light. Make them as descriptive as possible and use as many action verbs as you can: "led," "managed," "supervised," and "accomplished" are words that resonate with employers. Again, avoid any typographical or spelling errors. This demonstrates a lack of attention to detail that employers will take seriously.

Facebook

Facebook began as a way to connect people socially. As its use has exploded, people have come to see it as a platform to make both personal and professional contacts. There are two points of view about how your publicly accessible Facebook profile can impact your job search.

One view is that, when entering the internship or job market, you should "clean up" your profile, put your best digital foot forward, and present a professional, buttoned-down version of yourself on social media platforms. The other point of view is that people are people and *act like people*, and to hide this can be disingenuous. Again, there is much debate about "being yourself," but I recommend making private anything online that you think may even have the possibility of disqualifying you for a job. I have debated this with friends, but it's like going to an interview; you put your best foot forward. This means dressing professionally, having an interesting and informative resume, and being on time. Don't give potential employers the opportunity to disqualify you before or during the process. That is the equivalent of wearing jeans to an interview, showing up late, and chewing gum.

Creating a professional profile on Facebook that is completely visible is easy. The only difference between this profile and your personal profile is the email address. You can have the same name, but Facebook bases its accounts on email addresses. So go out, get yourself another Gmail or Yahoo! email address and start putting together your professional profile. I have several friends who have done this and their professional Facebook profiles include:

- A professional profile picture (just like on LinkedIn)
- Timelines posts or Notes that reflect thoughts, opinions, and links to other sources of information about a topic—in this case, social media. For example, you could post links to the latest Mashable (www.mashable.com) articles that interest you and leave a thoughtful comment about your take on the topic.
- Pictures of you that present you in a professional light, such as at networking events or working
- Under the Info tab, details about your education, career, and other insights that show that you are interested in or knowledgeable about a topic
- Good privacy settings. Choose who you want to be able to access to your Facebook profile by updating your privacy settings. At time of writing, simply use the dropdown menu in the upper right-hand corner of the Facebook dashboard. For example, you may only want your Facebook friends to be able to see your photos and status updates, rather than anyone on Facebook.

Third-Party Facebook Apps that Can Help You Promote Yourself
There are services and apps that enable you to turn your Facebook page into an online resume. One of the easiest that I have discovered is BranchOut (www.branchout.com). BranchOut is an application that you use in conjunction with your existing Facebook profile. You begin by installing the app, giving it permission to access your Facebook

account, and then adding information either via LinkedIn or by uploading a copy of your resume. When you are through completing your profile, BranchOut gives you a Facebook-like page that presents much of the same information as LinkedIn, including your profile picture, name, career and educational history, people in your network, updates, and endorsements. If this seems pretty similar to LinkedIn, I imagine that its creators designed it to be just that: a LinkedIn competitor. The only difference is that you can build a network based upon your Facebook friends, and not those in your LinkedIn profile.

Mike DelPonte, marketing manager for BranchOut.com, told me that the benefits of using this app include the ability to create "profiles do not show personal information like status updates and photo albums. Rather, they display one professional photo of your choice, your work history, education, and endorsements from your friends and colleagues.[xix]"

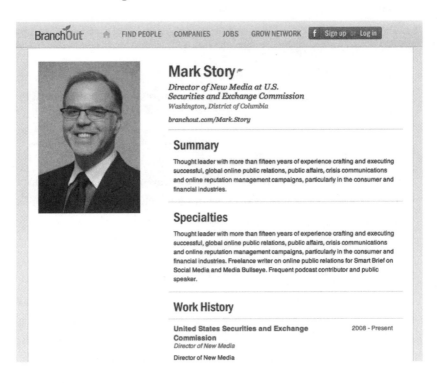

As Mike mentioned, what's interesting about BranchOut is that it strips away much of what could be considered to be embarrassing information or could lead to disqualification for a job. It does not import Timeline updates (you post your own updates on it, which would presumably be of a more professional nature), and it also has places for projects and endorsements (just like LinkedIn). It does not import any photos except for your profile picture. In short, BranchOut appears to be an "idiot-proof" tool that presents employer-worthy information while removing things from your profile that you may not want on it. Plus, if you are an employer, you can add open jobs to the network as well.

Finally, what I find most interesting is that the app has a link for "People You Should Know," suggestions for other BranchOut users with whom you should connect to further your professional network.

Another interesting app—and it appears to be more of a subsection on Facebook—is Marketplace (apps.facebook.com/marketplace/). It's a section where you can buy or sell items—or market yourself. Within the Marketplace is a jobs section. As an experiment, in the field "What type of job are you looking for?" I entered "social media" (with the quotes), and the search returned an astounding 2,466 job results. Granted, I did not specific a geographic region to narrow my search results to local opportunities—I saw jobs that were listed all over the United States—but a scan of the results showed some pretty interesting jobs. I clicked on one and saw that it is easy to both find and apply for jobs using this app.

The sample job that I came up with was a position as an interactive and social media manager for a company in New York. The Marketplace page also enabled me to:

- share the job using email, Facebook share, Twitter, or Google+;
- ask the person who posted the job a question or leave a comment;
- indicate interest by clicking on a button;
- ask the employer who posted the position if the job was still available; and
- read a detailed job description.

All of these elements are what you want out of the world's most visible social networking platform to learn about and apply for jobs. The key aspect of this is *social networking*. You are connecting on social levels by joining the same community and networking for jobs.

Other Good Ways to Use Facebook to Market Yourself

In a *Social Media Examiner* blog post,[xx] author Linda Coles also suggests creating a business Facebook profile—instead of a personal one—to market oneself for a job. This is an interesting concept if you approach your job as marketing yourself and you as your biggest client. You then become the product that you are trying to sell.

Coles suggests that you use your Facebook business profile as a blog: "[W]rite posts in the Notes tab about your thoughts and opinions of your industry. For example, if you're a marketer, maybe write about how you would approach a particular brand's campaign, or what you think worked or didn't work about a campaign. Use the Notes tab as a way of blogging." She also suggests running Facebook ads—for yourself. For what she describes as "a few dollars a day," you can "write yourself a nifty ad stating that you're looking for a position in your chosen field. If you're in marketing, this should give you free rein to write a creative ad to promote yourself. Facebook ads can be targeted to show up only on members' pages in a particular city, along with a whole lot of other targeting criteria."

There are other tactics that you can employ to make a publicly accessible Facebook profile a good tool to promote yourself. Use your personal or company page to announce to the world that you are looking for a job. Post frequent status updates that either provide progress information on your search (try to omit those that express frustration—you can save those for your private Facebook profile) like "Filled out an online application today for an entry-level social media job at eBay. Does anyone know anyone over there so I can get a sense of the corporate culture, or the sort of candidates they are looking for?" Something as simple as this status update may get you valuable contacts as well.

Speaking of contacts, "Like" the company pages of employers that you are targeting. First, they will show up in your Facebook feed and you can stay up-to-date on news about the company, but second, they just may post job openings on their Facebook page that will appear in your news feed. People within the company you "Like" may notice you, your interest, and your job search, and may perhaps friend you, connecting you to someone within the company who could assist with your job search.

At the Securities and Exchange Commission in 2011, I created a Facebook page whose sole purpose is to gain followers and publicize job openings that people may not otherwise know about. Especially when it comes to working in government, it is very difficult to find where to look for and apply for a job. By creating this page (www.facebook.com/SECJobs), I put the jobs where people already are: on the largest social networking platform in the world. I also created a Twitter account that lists the same job openings (@SEC_Jobs). Both have greatly helped expand the reach and scope of our recruitment efforts.

Make and Post a Video Resume

Many bands and other online personalities have established and earned online fame and cult followings with compelling YouTube videos (think "Annoying Orange," www.annoyingorange.com). Why not create one of your own? It's not hard to do, and a quick, ninety-second recitation about you, your accomplishments, and your professional goals is a terrific way to set yourself apart from other candidates. It can be as easy as sitting in front of your computer and recording with the webcam on it, then saving and uploading the video to YouTube.

While it is not scientific, a quick YouTube search for "my video resume" returned 30,500 results. On the first page of search results, I found "My Awesome Video Resume" by Justin McNurdo.[xxi] He begins his video with a blank screen, providing only his name and phone number, and then, in a very funny way, a narrator talks about Justin's work attributes (this may well be a parody, but it's still funny and effective).

Others suggest video resumes as well. In his blog post "How many people are using YouTube to post video resumes?" The Resume Bear suggests[xxii]:

○ Using the words "video resume" will increase the chances of your video resume being found.

- ° Checking to see if there are video resumes on YouTube that are similar to your background and industry. If so, "take note of the keywords they use to describe their video. Why? If someone sees their resume, it's a good chance that they will discover yours as a 'related video.'"

Your Next Marketing Tools: Your Writing and Your Blog

Information that can be perceived as positive or negative by potential employers goes beyond information that they find on Facebook. If you blog and are seeking a job in which you will do so in a professional capacity, your own blog needs to have good grammar and be error-free, as well as being attractive and easy to read. The content on your blog should be the best representation of the writing that you would do for an employer, so the quality of your grammar could be an indication of how seriously you take things like proofreading. As I mentioned in prior chapters, the ability to express yourself using the written word is critical. If your blog is poorly written and is full of incomplete sentences and grammatical mistakes, you are sending a message to both your readers and to potential employers that you do not pay attention to detail—a critical success factor for any job.

Make Your Bones

One of my favorite television shows is Anthony Bourdain's *No Reservations*. Bourdain is a former chef, author, and now TV host who is funny, profane, and insightful, and makes very good television.

I suspect that his profane and sarcastic nature comes from working as a chef or in kitchens for nearly thirty years. One of his favorite expressions about working is that you have to "make your bones." This phrase means to work hard and earn respect in a field, and he's constantly pointing to chefs who have "made their bones."

If you want to "make your bones" in social media, blog about social media. Find a list of blogs or topics that interest you. Read them. Comment on them. Do the same with Twitter. Find people who post interesting links. Follow them and interact with them on Twitter. This will help you build your own Twitter following. Start discussions on Google+. In short, show the world of social media that you get it: that you are intellectually curious and have opinions and ideas and can express them well, and that you know the tools and how to use them. Share all of this on your Facebook page. This will also create an online record of the fact that you can "make your bones" in social media.

How Your Expressed Opinions Mesh with Those of Potential Future Employers

When you are looking for a job and creating social media profiles, as well as interacting with others via tweets, Facebook wall posts, or blog comments, you are expressing opinions. These opinions are creating what may well be a permanent record of what or how you think. This can be good and bad.

Evan Kraus of APCO Worldwide told me, "It's about common sense. I tend to look at candidates' online presence, and if they have done something that I consider unprofessional or not smart or well reasoned, that sends me a pretty strong signal of their level of judgment."[xxiii] Robert French of Auburn University told me that younger people need to "earn the right" to criticize things and people online.[xxiv]

Information that may cause employers to pause may also involve opinions that you have expressed that could be counter to theirs or those of their clients. If you are applying to an agency whose main client in Microsoft and your blog is full of anti-Microsoft rants, you may want to consider not applying for the position, or if you can put your views aside, removing these posts from your blog (with the understanding that others may have blogged about your views and you can't erase everything online). The same is true with tweets; if you have posted repeatedly that you hate tobacco companies, and the agency that is your potential employer does work with R. J. Reynolds Tobacco Company—even if you don't do work on the account—removing the tweets may not be enough. It is possible that others may have retweeted your opinions and listed your Twitter handle on their own accounts. It may be something like "@mstory123 really went on about how he hates the tobacco companies." When, as is true in almost all social media, you cannot control the dissemination of information, even if it is about you, think carefully about what you put online that may impact your future career. The Internet is forever.

It's Not Just about Facebook and Twitter—They Googled You

It's a bit dated, but a June 2007 edition of the *Harvard Business Review* puts forth the case "We Googled You"[xxv] and discusses a fictitious job candidate, Mimi Brewster, who is applying for a job working for a clothing manufacturer in Shanghai, China. An overzealous human resources manager who was at odds with the company's CEO and his fondness for Mimi searched for and found information on page nine (PAGE NINE!) of a Google search that indicated that Mimi, while studying at Stanford, had been involved in student protests that could, if discovered by their Chinese suppliers, cause problems for their company:

> It was soon clear that Mimi's involvement had been more than just a student's expression of defiance. One newspaper story featured a photo of Mimi sitting outside China's San Francisco consulate protesting China's treatment of a dissident journalist.[xxvi]

This is a fictitious example, but one that brings up the point that online information that could damage your chances at employment can be more than Facebook keg stands and tweets. Even though it is buried in Google, if people want to find it, they will find it. Consider this carefully when you begin to market yourself to potential employers. What is out there that potential employers could find about you, your background, and your opinions?

As I mentioned, the flip side of this is being yourself—presenting yourself as a "real person," whether you are twenty and in college or thirty and advancing in the work force. If you believe strongly either for or against something and choose to participate in a protest, go for it. But in so doing (especially if you write about it or have your picture taken and tagged), know that it is out there for anyone to see, and without some time-consuming and intensive scrubbing, it will likely follow you for the rest of your career.

The alternative opinion to exposing one's views in a very public fashion—and leaving them there for the world to see—was expressed by digital practitioner and blogger Antonia Harler: (her blog is www. socialglitz.com and her Twitter account is @antoniaharler). Antonia believes that employers hire real people with real lives—and many young people drink, go to parties, and sometimes do keg stands. "While it's important to be careful about what you put up there, every company is run by humans. If the decision to hire you is based upon one or two stupid pictures on Facebook, I don't know if I want to work for you."[xxvii] She is fine with people discovering facts about her life and has been open on her blog about her successes, her failures, and some deeply personal issues. She added, "If you want to find dirt on someone, you will find dirt, no matter how secure your online profile is. You can control your own pictures on Facebook, but you might not remember that people tag you on their Facebook pictures."

The decision to lock down, clean up, or keep public your activities, thoughts, and opinions is yours, but think carefully about the potential ramifications as you build your own online portfolio to market to employers.

Expert Insight: Building Your Personal Brand; 300 Words that Changed My Life[xxviii]:

Antonia Harler, social media strategist at Paratus Communications, London

Q: How did your studies prepare you for a career in social media? How has your education prepared you?
A: It didn't prepare me for a career in social media. I am self-taught. My education is in management and IT. I did a semester in the United States at the City College of New York. I took a PR course and it frightened me because I

am not a native English speaker. The course had nothing to do with my degree and was all writing—press releases, etc. It turned out that I was top of the class and I was very impressed with my teacher. Public relations interested me greatly. We talked about social media and blogging, but I did not know how to use Twitter or do a blog.

There was no one to teach me about social media, so the only way had to learn it was by buying books like the *Social Media Bible* and others and teaching myself. But you are only going to learn it by doing it.

Q: Tell me about the blog post that changed your life.

A: Three hundred words changed my life: unbelievable, right? I planned a trip to London for two weeks, and I went to job interviews almost every day. . . . Two weeks later, I went back home—frustrated—because people said, "You're amazing but you have no experience." How could I get experience without being offered a job or an internship?

I had three glasses of wine before I wrote my blog post. I built a blog that had a decent readership— I poured everything in there. There were facts, but there was also a lot of personal information in the post. When I was doing my dissertation on Twitter and customer relationship management, I got in touch with a wide variety of people in the social media space—people with big followings, so I sent twenty emails that were pleas. I asked for a tweet, a Facebook/LinkedIn update, or anything to help me, really. It was such a long shot, but I had to try it. All twenty helped me in one way or another. In three days, the blog post was read by more than one thousand people and my inbox was flooded with hundreds of emails. It was literally my last shot at getting a job.

One day, I was out for coffee with my friends and my phone buzzed with a direct message on Twitter from my current boss. All he said was, "I have a freelance job for you if you are interested." I messaged him back. And he said, "When can you start?"

Q: For people who are considering making the same leap that you did, what advice would you give them? A: Don't compromise on what you believe in. I felt like a failure, but I did not compromise. Even if you don't have the experience, you can work hard and prove that you can work hard. Be active in social media. Walk the walk. Have a blog and a Twitter account—if you don't have the experience, you need to have a social media presence and understand that if you don't have the experience you need to convince potential bosses another way and that is by showing them what you can do. Treat your job hunt like a mini social media campaign. Consider all aspects of it. Research (lots and lots of research), blogger outreach, advertising, maybe even write a press release and reach out to newspapers. Some efforts may seem ridiculous, but remember the one who doesn't try already failed.

Summary

Whether you are working in a kitchen like Anthony Bourdain did or in social media, you need to "make your bones." What's great about social media, however, is that you can (and should) openly publicize your good work.

The beauty of looking for a job in social media is that there are many, many free platforms to demonstrate to potential employers that you can "walk the walk" when it comes to being a polished candidate for a junior position. Investigate, read, write, know the tools, and put your best online foot forward.

CHAPTER 4

MAKING YOURSELF
VISIBLE TO EMPLOYERS

"A whopping 36.6 million Americans say that they got their current job via social media: 18.4 million Americans say they got their current job via Facebook, 8 million via Twitter, and 10.2 million via LinkedIn. These people account for 16 percent of all employees, up from 11 percent in 2010."[xxix]

These statistics demonstrate what many people already know; millions are using social media to get on the radar of potential employers. If you "practice what you preach" to prepare yourself for a career in social media, you will have a built-in advantage over others in the job market: you will have highly visible, attractive sites that showcase your social media know-how.

Expert Insight: The Importance of Being a Social Media Practitioner

Trying to start a career—or even get a job—in social media without first mastering the tools for personal use is, at best, foolish. Again, you have to "practice what you preach." There is a big leap between making use of a social media platform for personal use and turning it into a career in which you give advice, but many of those whom I interviewed for the book had equally strong feelings about teaching yourself as much as you can about the medium by *using the tools*. Using these tools will help (a) make you more visible, and (b) create an online portfolio for potential employers to evaluate. Two experts below both believe that if you are applying for a job in social media, you must first "walk the walk":

- *David Almacy, former Internet and e-communications director at the White House:* "If you have an interest in digital, you should be a personal advocate of it. Use the technology . . . It's about being visible both online and offline. Start a blog and write about something that's happening in the social media world and what you think about. It shows me that you understand how the social media works. I can bring you in and teach you corporate communications or public affairs, or how to strategically think about in the way that we present that to clients. But you have shown that you have some curiosity about social media."[xxx]

- *Chuck DeFeo, former e-campaign manager for Bush/Cheney '04:* "You have to engage in the medium in which you want to work. You have to be on Facebook (I have interviewed people who are not). The best advice I would give to people I got from my basketball coach in grade school. Practice doesn't make perfect; perfect practice makes perfect. You have to understand what it is you are trying to accomplish—you are a communicator and a lot of people can go out and just because they have a Facebook profile page, believe that they are an effective social media communicator. There are not a lot of opportunities to take courses in something like at the class [the author] used to teach at Georgetown. You have to use the tools personally that you plan on using professionally."[xxxi]

- *Antonia Harler, Paratus Communications:* "Be active in social media. Walk the walk. Have a blog and a Twitter account—if you don't have the experience, you need to have a social media presence and understand that if you don't have the experience you need to convince potential bosses another way, and that is by showing them what you can do. Treat your job hunt like a mini social media campaign. Consider all aspects of it."[xxxii]

- *Evan Kraus, executive vice president and director, APCO Online:* "You have to be a practitioner to be good at giving clients advice. You need to have your own presence at one level. Horror stories—keep it professional and understand the ramifications of trashing brands. It's about common sense. I tend to look at candidates' online presence, and if they have done something that I consider unprofessional or not smart or well reasoned, that sends me a pretty strong signal of their level of judgment."[xxxiii]

Making yourself visible to employers by engaging the media in which you want to work will not only give you the exposure you need in front of prospective employers, but also teach you some of the fundamental social media skills that you can later refine for work in a professional environment. It's a must.

More about Making Yourself Visible

I covered this in chapter 3, "Applying Your Experience," but it is worth repeating. Creating an online body of work by being a social media user will help you *get the interview*. It doesn't matter if you are starting out looking for a job, are a midlevel practitioner looking to advance your career, or are a seasoned professional: you need to have an online portfolio that people can easily find when they Google you. And note that I said "*when* they Google you" and not "*if* they Google you." It is almost certain that potential employers will look you up and find your LinkedIn profile, your Facebook personal page (or business page as one expert suggested in chapter 3), your blog, and other online tools that you have used to establish your online voice, like a Twitter or Pinterest account or Google+ profile. In short, what you need to do is to make it easy for employers to find you.

There are three good ways to accomplish this: build as many sites as are practical to create an online body of work that people can easily find, use good search engine optimization in your online profiles to help hiring people find you, and list all of your social media properties on your resume.

Creating Additional Online Properties

As I have mentioned, the more sites that link back to yours, the better, so be creative about how you market yourself. Many websites enable you to create posts that contain links back to your site *and* further publicize what you have written—just in different places. For example, when you write something that you want to broadcast online, consider using:

- *Twitter*: since you are presumably already posting links to others' content and commenting on it, be sure to post links to your own work. Moreover, as you follow other Twitter users and hopefully they follow you back, read their content. Absorb it. If you think that it is of interest to people who follow you (or may in the future), re-tweet it and provide a short commentary and link in your own profile.

The most common convention for doing this is by identifying it as a share (a re-tweet), listing its author, and offering quick summary as well as a shortened link. This might look something like this: "RT @mstory123 'Job Seeking is a Double-Edged Sword' - bit.ly/vFXe09." Since Twitter will only accept 140 characters, some people use a link-shortening service like bit.ly.com or tinyurl.com.

When you participate in an online conversation that is discussing a post, an idea, or an issue, you are creating an online record of your thoughts and opinions. This is exactly the sort of footprint that potential employers will be interested in reading. And with a little luck, others who follow you on Twitter may find value in your tweets and re-tweet them as well, creating additional links to your content.

- *LinkedIn*: In addition to the benefits outlined in chapter 3, "Applying Your Experience," LinkedIn also has a very prominent place in your profile where you can share an update and a link. Post a link to your latest blog post, tweet, or Google+ update! It will not only draw links back to your original blog post or page, but also add to your online portfolio. Don't forget to add links to others' content that you find meaningful as well.

- *RSS* (Really Simple Syndication): RSS is simply a format that enables you to automatically package the content from your blog or your website into a feed that you broadcast and is easy for people to import and read. Many blogging platforms like WordPress and Tumblr (a multimedia-oriented blogging platform: people post lots of pictures and videos) have built-in RSS feeds. By automatically converting your content to an RSS feed, you make it more visible for those who use RSS readers.

Helping Them Find You: Search Engine Optimization

Referred to as "SEO" by many industry practitioners, "search engine optimization" sounds fancy, but it is simply a way to make it easy to find information about you—adding content and code in order to improve visibility within Google.

And note that I use the word "Google" rather than "in search engines." Despite their efforts, Microsoft's Bing search engine still comprises only 4.24 percent of all searches. In comparison, 76 percent of searches are carried out with Google.[xxxiv, xxxv] That does not suggest that you should ignore Bing or Yahoo (at 5.55 percent), but I would encourage you simply to submit your sites to them (it's quick and easy) and be done with it, focusing instead on the nearly eight out of ten people who use Google.

What's in a Name—in Google?

In the many, many speeches I've given, when Google comes up, I always point out that it reached prominence for me when it went from a noun to a verb: you now *Google* something or someone. It's that important now, and not just in our lexicon—it's how we discover things.

With this is mind, if you want to promote yourself online, you need to establish a search term that is closely associated with your name or for your name itself. For example, I have made efforts to link my name with the phrase "starting a career in social media" as well as "Mark Story." Your name is your brand. When potential employers Google you, they will be looking for *you*: information about you and for many of the facets mentioned in chapter 3, "Applying Your Experience," such as views, opinions, online portfolios, pictures, and writing.

Placement Matters

Please also note that I consistently refer to the first page in Google search results, because if you are not there, you don't matter (leaving aside sponsored search terms).

- One source[xxxvi] reports that 91 percent of searchers do not go past page one of the search results, and over 50 percent do not go past the first three results on page one.

- Another study[xxxvii] broke down not only who goes to page two of search results, but how likely it was that users would click on links on the first page:

Position on Page	Percent of All Clicks
1	45.46
2	15.69
3	10.09
4	5.49
5	5.00
6	3.94
7	2.51
8	2.94
9	1.97
10	2.71

The statistics above indicate that not only are you virtually invisible if you show up on page two of a Google search (95.91 percent of all clicks occur on page one), but *where* you show up on the first page matters a great deal as well. So even if you build an awesome online brand or set of fantastic websites, unless someone is willing to dig to find information about you, you need to be on the first page to matter. Caveat: if your name is "John Smith," or another a common name, you may have some hurdles to jump over and need to find other search terms that will help distinguish you.

Many "Storys" to Recount: An Example of SEO

So as not to embarrass anyone but myself, let's use the example of my name as it relates to visibility in Google. It surprised me when I first looked, but there is more than one Mark Story out there, and the first page of search results in Google reveals that there are Mark Storys who are not this author. I have invested enough time and effort to appear in six of the top ten search results for my name in Google, but other Mark Storys out there include a photographer (markstoryphotography.com), a technical blogger (mark-story.com) and a sportswriter for the *Lexington Herald Leader* (Kentucky). Since I began building my online brand in the hopes of furthering my career, as well as expressing myself, I have considered myself to be in competition with the other Mark Storys for precious real estate on the first page of Google and have used some basic tactics of SEO to help elevate my Google search engine ranking.

These "Mark Story competitors" have some built-in advantages, including:

- The sites' web addresses. One of the main, if not the *most*, important factor to ensure your name shows up on the first page of Google search results is the wording that appears in your URL (the fancy term is "universal resource locator"), or your web address. So mark-story.com and markstoryphotography.com have built-in advantages because Google thinks that the information listed here is very relevant—it's in the web address after all, so it has to be relevant. And Google indexes the sites this way, giving them prominence.

- The number of web pages associated with them. The sportswriter for the *Lexington Herald Leader* writes for a newspaper (these are generally frequently visited sites) and writes often. So the more columns that this Mark Story churns out, the more his name appears in the search engine rankings both for the newspaper site's visibility as well as for the frequency with which his name appears in the columns. So if he churns out 200 columns a year, he has 200 pages for Google to index. Nice advantage.

What I Have Done to Crawl to the Top

You'll note that, in the graphic and as I have mentioned above, I have the top four spots in Google and six of the top ten search results—despite the built-in advantages that the other Mark Storys have. This is because I have worked in and around the field of search engine optimization for some time and know a few tricks that help me (and can help you) appear in the first page of Google search results. These include:

- Google is in love with Google. The first two results are my public Google profile and my Google+ profile. Presumably, Google thinks that the information that it presents is the most relevant and important, so the simple task of creating these profiles makes them appear at the top of search engine results.

- Google loves *meaningful* repetition, and uses it as part of the mysterious and ever-changing algorithm that they use to rank sites. Google, like Santa, knows if you are naughty or nice. It figures out if (a) you are spamming a word within your pages ("Amy Winehouse, Amy Winehouse, Amy Winehouse, Amy Winehouse, Amy Winehouse, Amy Winehouse") without having words around it that provide context (this is known as "content farming," and they penalize for it by pushing you lower in their rankings), or (b) you have genuine, multiple uses of a word, like those listed below (Google likes this). Using the "nice" method is called "keyword density."

Use Easy Tools to Make You More Visible

Additional links from search engine results on the first page of Google come from one of my blogs, *The Intersection of Online and Offline*, which I created for the course I taught at Georgetown University: www.intersectionofonlineandoffline.com. You'll note that the page title (the words that appear at the top of your browser on every page) has "Mark Story's Intersection of Online and Offline." I inserted my name into the title to ensure that Google reads it on every page and registers it: more keyword density. Google is OK with this.

You don't need to be an expert or a programmer to have good search engine optimization; you just need access to the right tools. For all of my websites, I use WordPress, which is a blogging and website development platform (sort of for dummies—it takes about an hour to get a a professional-looking and easy-to-maintain website up and running).

What All-in-One SEO Pack Can Do for You

One of the best things about WordPress is that there are thousands of plug-ins (small programs that you can add to your site) that can help you do what you want to, like add social bookmarking links, as we discussed previously, or other tactics to promote your site. WordPress has an excellent free plug-in called All in One SEO Pack (wordpress.org/ extend/plugins/all-in-one-seo-pack/) that enables you to add items that Google thinks are important and insert them into the code on your page—the code that Google reads and indexes. For the purposes of this book, I refer to "code" as words that are invisible to you and your readers, but that matter greatly to search engines like Google.

It's easy to create code using this program. After your write the text of your post, there are fields that you fill in for the post title, a summary (the first couple of lines that appear in Google search results—a good description helps people determine what is on the page and make the decision to click on it or not) and, finally, keywords. Keywords are descriptive terms that show up in the code of the page which Google will then read. So with some copying and pasting, you have just added code that is vital to what Google thinks is important. And you don't have to be a programmer to do it. The beauty of plug-ins is that you don't need to be an expert to use them; you just need to understand their importance.

If You Love SEO, Avoid Blogger

If search engine optimization matters to you, I would avoid using the blogging platform Blogger (blogger.com). Blogger is one of the quickest and easiest tools to build and launch a blog (and it's one of the few that are still free), but it is virtually devoid of any tools that can help you with search engine optimization. There are almost no plug-ins, and aside from the ability to create some tags for each post, if you select this platform, you will find that your options are limited when it comes to creating some of the important elements to have your site gain a premier position in Google, like page descriptions, title tags, and meta tags.

Why I Use Search Engine Optimization Tools

I use these tools for all of my websites not because of ego, but because they are part of my online arsenal to ensure that people who are looking for me can quickly and easily find me—and to keep one step ahead of those other Mark Storys! Good search engine optimization has helped get me to—and keep me at—the top of Google search results. It takes time and effort, but as you build your own career, it can pay off when information about you that matters to employers is easy to find, professional, and shows that you can "walk the walk" when it comes to social media.

Other Easy-to-Use Plug-Ins to Help Share Your Content

When you use do-it-yourself website and blogging platforms like WordPress, Blogger, or Tumblr, there are thousands of other nifty, free plug-ins or built-in tools that can help you spread the word about your site and its pages.

Social Bookmarking Services

Many blogging platforms have built-in tools that help people share content based on "social bookmarking services" like Digg, Delicious, Reddit, and others. Simply put, social bookmarking means that you establish an account on one of these services like Digg (digg.com), and when you encounter something that you think is of value—you are bookmarking it with others in mind—you click on the Digg icon, get a pop-up window, type a few words about the link that you are providing, and you have created a link on another website.

As you'll note from the image below, which comes from a guest blog post I did, many bloggers list the most popular bookmarking and sharing tools (in this case, Facebook, Google+, Twitter, LinkedIn, and Pinterest) and make it easy for people who like their posts to share them with others.

Using social bookmarking services is a good way to promote your own writing because (a) you can create additional links back to your own content, drawing more attention to your own online work, and (b) by using a third-party website, you are creating an online record of which content you think is interesting or important—one that future potential employers can find and check out as well.

One final note about plug-ins and add-ons: like many social media platforms, popular social bookmarking services come and go. It's critical to stay on top of which bookmarking sites are popular and which are not, and to find the tool that presents the best opportunity to publicize your page.

Your Work Is Done (Sort Of)

While the job of establishing and, more importantly, maintaining a social media presence is never quite finished, if you have accomplished the steps laid out in this chapter, you have likely created a strong online presence—one that will eventually attract the attention of employers. Someone will find your information or you will apply for a job and have already constructed a solid body of work from which employers can judge you.

It's time to turn the page to how potential employers will begin to view and evaluate the information that they find about you. This is called the "screening process."

How the Job Screening Process Works

We'll cover more of how employers search for candidates in chapter 5, "Using Social Media to Land the Right Interview for the Right Job," but since you have done the work to create an online portfolio and "put yourself out there," you can be sure that potential employers will view your information. Finding the right job takes time and patience, but it begins with the screening process.

"Back in the day" (which is a middle-aged person's euphemism for before something ubiquitous existed, as explained to people who know nothing else), most people found jobs via the newspaper. It was a straightforward yet wildly mysterious and uncertain process. You scanned the want ads in a print newspaper, circled the ones you thought sounded like they might be right, and did what the ad instructed. You sent in a resume, a writing sample, a salary history, and sometimes professional or personal references. Employers also became more sophisticated and tacked on something to their ads: "No calls, please." And then you waited. And waited. And waited.

I worked in the employment industry from 1987 until 1995, and for most of my time in the field as a recruiter for other companies, that's how the process worked. We would put an ad in the paper and wait for the deluge of resumes or phone calls. I would never say this at the time, but my opinion was—and still is—that the first phase of recruitment is *a search for the negative*. You read that right: not a search for the right candidate, but a search for the negative.

Think about it: especially for entry-level positions, the person who initially receives and sorts through the first batch of resumes is usually inundated with candidate information. It's human nature to want to weed through the dozens or hundreds of resumes as quickly as possible. That usually begins by eliminating those candidates who simply don't meet the requirements. That's why I say that the first phase is a search for the negative. If a recruiter's job is to find the diamond, one must first sort through a lot of layers of earth. And the faster that person can sort through the earth, the better. Hence, the search for the negative to make the pile of resumes get smaller and smaller. This is how the screening process begins.

This is not to say that frontline recruiters (or "screeners") do not and will not identify good candidates. But the fact is that for every entry-level position, there are likely more candidates who are not qualified than those who are. That human being on the other end of the email, online form, LinkedIn mail, or however you are sending your information is wading through the first batch *searching for the negative* to get to the positive—the right candidates. And this is where first impressions matter. You want to put yourself in a position to make a good, very quick, and lasting impression, and to make the individual who is screening to put your resume in the pile of potential candidates.

When putting your resume together, don't forget to add links to your social media properties *at the top of your resume,* just below your contact information. Make it easy for recruiters to learn more about you.

Summary

Now that you have established an online presence made up of profiles that demonstrate that you have an online expertise, it's a lot easier to convince prospective employers that you can provide valuable insight about social media in a professional environment. You still need to look for and find a job, however—hopefully one that becomes a career. This is no easy task. What's hard for many to grasp, however, especially in this field, is that very few people have educational preparation; most have joined the world of social media by simply reading, doing, and learning.

In the next chapter, "Using Social Media to Land the Right Interview for the Right Job," I'll lay out how you can use social media to move from the screening process to the interview process, with the help of online tools and strategies.

CHAPTER 5

USING SOCIAL MEDIA TO LAND THE RIGHT INTERVIEW FOR THE RIGHT JOB

"Inevitably, I think, the Internet will divide job-hunters into two separate 'classes.' The first class will be those who have access to the Internet, and who are in fields whose employers use the Internet for their hiring process, and who have skills which the Internet prizes, and who find themselves in great demand. The other class will be those who either do not have access to the Internet, or who are in fields whose employers do not use the Internet for their hiring process, or who are job-hunters who have skills which the Internet does not particularly prize in its job-listings, and who consequently are not in great demand on the Internet." —Richard N. Bolles, author of *What Color Is Your Parachute? A Practical Manual for Job-Hunters and Career-Changers*[xxxviii]

As the quote above describes, if you are a social media practitioner, you already have a leg up on the competition. It's one thing to have *access* to the Internet as Bolles lays out, but it's another (and better) thing to have mastered some of the ways to promote yourself to employers along your path of building a career in social media.

If You Build It, They Will Come

Now that you have established your own online body of work, it's time to reverse your thinking a bit. In prior chapters, our work was somewhat passive. We covered building online platforms like blogs and Twitter accounts and waiting for the world to come by and hire us. What we'll cover in this chapter is how those same tools can turn passive job searches ("if you build it, [they] will come") into active job hunts.

The people behind social networks like LinkedIn and Facebook are smart. They have gone beyond enabling people to connect for the purpose of merely being social; they have turned their websites into platforms to perform vigorous job searches. Instead of promoting yourself to employers and waiting for them to pick you, I urge you to use many of these sites to instead *pick a future employer.*

Finding the Right Employer: Playing Detective

By now, you already have a sense of how important it is to find the right place to work. No method is 100 percent foolproof, but investigating in the beginning can help identify—and also eliminate—some prospective employers. As I mentioned before, the employment and interview process is a two-way street. You are checking them out (or should be) just as much as your potential future employer is checking you out. Don't forget that a company might sound like a dream to work for, but turn out to be a nightmare.

I remember talking to a colleague when I worked at Fleishman-Hillard who did work for a professional baseball team in the Midwest. I am a baseball fanatic, so I expressed to him how great I thought it would be to do client work for a baseball team. He indicated that it was "a nightmare," and that, although he entered into work excited to live out his passion as a baseball fan, it was such a negative experience that it almost ruined his love for baseball. This was a real wake-up call for me. In short, all that glitters is not gold—even a company or person whom you might think would be a dream employer may not be as advertised. Or worse. You have to do your research.

Proactive Job Hunting: Targeting Companies, Non-Job-Specific Openings

There are two basic ways to find a job: proactive and reactive. You can target employers who are attractive to you regardless of any posted job openings (proactive), or you can apply for advertised, open positions (reactive).

If you want to take the proactive approach, you'll be doing a lot of research: research about locations, company culture, and potential fits within companies that you target. Start by thinking about employers whose industry or clients may interest *you,* and then do some investigation. If you know people who work there (or are connected to them on social media platforms like Linke-dIn), ask them about the job environment. Talk to other friends about their jobs and where they like working; read online reviews of the top employers either in the country or where you live. Look for employee testimonials or reviews. In short, pick the places where you want to work and target them.

Tactic #1: Make Good Use of "Best of" Lists

If a company appears on a list of "best places to work," you should strongly consider doing some homework to determine if your skill set and personality would be a good fit there. "Best of" lists do the homework for you. I live in the Washington, DC area, and each year, *Washingtonian* magazine publishes their list of the "50 Greatest Places to Work in Washington."[xxxix] They describe their winners as those who meet these criteria: "What makes a place to work something special? Is it good pay and benefits? A healthy balance between work and life? Smart colleagues? Or is it interesting work—and the freedom to do that work without being micromanaged? According to the 13,000 who filled out our Great Places to Work survey, it's all of the above. It's not easy to find an employer that offers all those things. These 50 workplaces do."

Resources like this are invaluable. When I worked for both APCO and Fleishman-Hillard, I went through the process of submitting information to *Washingtonian*—the surveys were anonymous questionnaires given to the employees of companies that chose to be evaluated. The bonus of exercises like this is that the information collected by those ranking the employers (and augmented by on-site visits by *Washingtonian* staff writers) comes directly from the employees and is largely devoid of company spin.

While I was at APCO, we made the list of the 50 Greatest Places to Work in Washington in 2005. My friend in human resources told me that the number of resumes that we received that year increased by 2,000 from the prior year. It's very, very good advertising for the company as well.

One final note: APCO won the award in 2005, but out of 50 winners in Washington in 2011, we were the *only* communications and public relations firm to make the list. The only one. When I was in the agency business, several public relations, public affairs, or boutique social media firms would routinely make the list of the best places to work. I don't follow the list every year, but my friends who are still in the industry tell me that since the economic meltdown of 2008, pressure on employees to keep and attract new clients has increased exponentially, as has the pressure to perform, no matter what the challenge is. Pressure leads to stress, and for many, stress leads to less job satisfaction. This may be one of the reasons that several prominent PR agencies have dropped off the *Washingtonian* list.

More "Best of" Lists

You don't have to live in Washington, DC to research and find these sorts of lists. For example, *Crain's Business New York* produced a "Best Places to Work in New York in 2011"[xl] and CNN Money produced a nationwide 2011 list with 100 best companies to work for in each state.[xli] These are both excellent sources of information for your research.

Using Other Lists: Agency Report Cards

If you want to work for a public affairs or public relations agency that has a social media offering (almost all of the large-and medium-sized companies do), you can take advantage of other resources that do the work for you by providing a list of agencies and many times also offering reviews of the agency itself.

The Holmes Report. One such publication is The Holmes Report (holmesreport.com), produced by the Holmes Group, begun in 2000 by Paul Holmes. According to their website, they offer "annual Report Cards on the public relations business in North America, the EMEA (Europe, the Middle East and Africa) region, and Asia-Pacific, providing credible, independent profiles of more than leading

400 public relations firms each year."[xlii] In short, they rank agencies by the quality of the work that they do or the awards that they win. If you are interested in finding an agency that is profitable and does award-winning work, The Holmes Report is a good place to start because it offers such comprehensive resources.

When you read these lists, however, it's important to remember that people do these rankings, so the outcome can be both objective and subjective. When I worked at APCO Worldwide, Paul Holmes came to meet with our owner and talk to her and other senior agency executives for his annual agency report card. We all received an email in advance that he would be visiting. The implicit message was to watch what we said in the hallways and be on our best behavior. This is not to say that APCO was not deserving of the accolades that it received. When I worked there in 2003, APCO was named International Agency of the Year by The Holmes Report—no small feat. My point is that humans do agency rankings and they are highly subjective.

The Holmes Report also has a searchable agency directory that enables you to look up agencies by name or geographical location as well as by agency offerings like biotechnology, business-to-business, or cause marketing.[xliii] Or if you are interested in finding an agency that has a social media offering, you can list a city and select "digital communications" in the agency specialty field. Once you have located an agency that is near you and has a social media offering, you can continue your research.

Tactic #2: Choose a City, Then Choose an Employer

Washington, DC, where I live and work, is a transient city. Many people come and go and there are few "natives"—people who were born and raised there. I've met many people professionally who have come to Washington not for a particular job but to live in the city. Many said "I want to live in Washington, DC," then either made the move or found a job and then moved, but all had made up their minds that DC was the place to be. So to begin your career in social media, if you have the flexibility, you may want to move to a city where the jobs are.

In a February 2012 post on Ragan.com, author Kristin Piombino listed the top five cities for social media jobs in the United States, combined with information on what you will be likely to earn. So if you have not yet decided where you want to live to start your career in social media, here are some ideas[xliv]:
The top five cities with the most social media jobs are:

1. New York, New York
2. San Jose, California
3. San Francisco, California
4. Los Angeles, California
5. Boston, Massachusetts

Relocation is not for everyone, but if you aspire to kick-start your career in social media, you greatly enhance your chances of landing your dream job if you live in an area that is home to a great deal of social media jobs. Think of the example of Antonia Harler, whom we met in chapter 3: "Applying Your Experience." She chose her city first (London), did a lot of research on potential employers, hopped on a plane with a few euros in her pocket, and eventually landed a job as a social media strategist.

Tactic #3: Narrow Your Field of Potential Employers

Once you have found an agency or company that interests you—either on the "best of" lists, through an industry directory, or simply by choosing a city—you can begin the next phase of your research: investigating others' opinions of the company. Websites like GlassDoor (glassdoor.com) offer reviews (presumably by the company's employees) of companies and their work atmospheres. Sites like these are good resources, but like many other sites that reviews companies or products, the reviews are anonymous, so you can assume that the reviews include a combination of employees who have been asked to write good reviews by their supervisors, disgruntled employees looking to vent, and former employees who probably feel more free to be open. You'll get a mix of opinions, but I still think that sites like these should serve as part of your research.

Tactic #4: To Get Interviews, Get Social

The same social media tools listed in the preceding chapters, like RSS readers, will help you make connections and discover open jobs. Most organizations list their open positions on their websites, and now many also list them on Twitter, LinkedIn, Facebook, or services like Indeed.com and Monster.com. Again, you have a built-in advantage because you are a social media practitioner; it should be easy for you to use many of these tools because you will already have developed a comfort level with them. I suggest using some of the following social media platforms to help connect you with employers that have open jobs that are attractive to you:

RSS Feeds

Wouldn't it be great to wake up in the morning and find the *right* job opportunities waiting for you on your computer screen? Using an RSS reader can make this much easier. Many larger organizations, like my former employer, Fleishman-Hillard, not only list their career opportunities on their website, but they also provide an RSS feed. In the image below, you can see job listings from the Fleishman RSS feed that I accessed on April 2, 2012. You can plug the Fleishman jobs feed into a reader like Google Reader and have an automatically updated list of jobs appear daily, but you can also filter the jobs that appear by searching for particular keywords. Filtering the jobs using words like "social media" and "Palo Alto, California" can help you weed through the jobs that do or do not contain keywords that represent the type of job you are looking for, and is also a good way to narrow by location in case you are not willing or able to relocate to another city (or endure a horrendous commute).

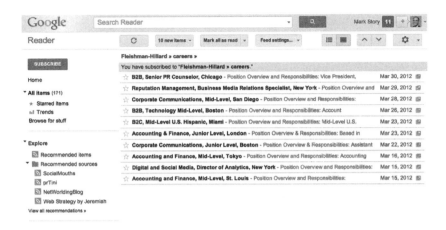

Step one for using an RSS reader is to establish an account using a service like Google Reader (google.com/reader). This is especially simple if you already have an account on Google, like Gmail or Google+. It takes minutes to set up. And after you have the account set up, you have a blank slate into which you can load RSS feeds—the jobs that may potentially interest you.

More RSS Feed Options: Aggregators

simply|hired.

Keywords

job title, skills or company

Location

city, state or zip

Search All Jobs

643,924 new jobs since your last visit

Find Jobs by Category

Accounting / Finance	Health Care / Nursing	Software / QA
Administrative / Clerical	Human Resources	Teaching
Architecture / Engineering	Legal / Paralegal	Truck Driving
Art / Graphic Design / Media	Marketing / PR / Advertising	Transportation / Logistics
Biotech / Science	Nonprofit / Volunteer	Writing / Freelance
Computer / Technology	Restaurant / Hotel	Part-time / Temporary
Customer Service	Retail	Summer / Seasonal
Executive / Management	Sales / Business Development	Entry Level / Internships

Browse Job Listings »

👍 Like   Be the first of your friends to like this.

Unlike Monster.com or CareerBuilder.com, job aggregator sites search thousands of resources that contain jobs and enable you to search by keywords, such as job title and location. One of my favorites is Simply Hired (simplyhired.com) because of its simplicity (no pun intended). To get started searching thousands of job sources, you enter your job title and the zip code of city where you want to work, and you are presented with a list of job that contain those keywords. When I did a search for "social media" and "Los Angeles, CA," the search returned 2,015 results. From those results, you can further refine them by job title, company, job type, required education and experience, and sources: job boards or recruiters. When you are through either using the simple keywords (job title and location) or some of the advanced filters, you can set up a daily or weekly alert to let you know when new jobs that match your criteria have been posted. It's easy and intuitive.

Indeed.com

Another good aggregator is Indeed.com. Like SimplyHired.com, Indeed.com provides a simple search (job title and city, state or zip code) as well as an advanced search in which you can filter jobs by including or excluding keywords, by company name, by job type (part-time, full-time, contract work), and by salary estimate as well as geography (the number of miles within the radius of the job location).

The beauty of Indeed.com is that you can turn your search results into an RSS feed, which you can then view in your RSS reader—it removes the manual step and can fit nicely into your RSS feed for job openings. Indeed.com also offers an email service which sends you an email when it finds jobs that meet the criteria that you defined.

Scary Monster

You might notice that I did not include the most well-known job search service, Monster.com. This site annoys me because of the plethora of advertising. At least two or maybe three times during the process of searching for jobs, pages that are actually ads (but cleverly altered to look like part of the site) appear when you are expecting to find pages that contain search results. Monster.com likely derives its revenue from both the fees that it charges companies as well as the advertising, but it annoys the heck out of me that I have to weed through the ads to get to the information that I want. Moreover, while you can sign up for email alerts that contain links to the jobs that meet your search criteria, there is no option for an RSS feed. Again, this indicates to me that they would rather you run the gauntlet of advertising than offer you direct access to the jobs that might be right for you.

If you are interested solely in jobs in the social media field, there are very specific and targeted resources like Jeremiah Owyang's Jobs for the Web Strategist site (web-strategist.com/blog) that aggregate just social media job openings from across the United States. Job for the Web Strategist does the work for you; Jeremiah finds the companies with openings in social media, adds them to an RSS feed, and publishes it, making it easy for you to import it into your own reader.

LinkedIn Jobs

 Digital Copywriter - Full Time Temporary Gig (that could convert to permanent)

Edelman - Washington, DC - Dec 7, 2011

▾ 2 connections can refer you to the job poster, A   B   2nd

 Senior Vice President at Edelman
1st

 MBA
20 Year Strategy, Marketing, Communication, Social Media, Brand, Digital, Advertising, Web, Sales, Publishing, Nonprofit
1st

In chapter 3, I spent a lot of time describing the benefits of using LinkedIn to create your *own* online profile and brand and network with people, but LinkedIn offers an additional, valuable benefit: you can use it as another active, online search resource to find jobs and sort them using a variety of criteria. Through your LinkedIn profile, you can search for jobs by title, geographical location, and company, but most importantly, by *relationships*. Again, LinkedIn does a lot of the work for you. You simply enter your job search criteria and the results that are displayed begin with the available jobs in companies where you already have connections on LinkedIn. Consider this: you have a much better chance of getting inside information on a job and/or getting a referral by knowing someone on the inside. LinkedIn not only makes this possible, but it makes it *easy*. The graphic that I included (I blurred the faces and deleted all of the names) shows that I have two "1st degree" or direct connections to people who work at Edelman in Washington, DC, the company that has advertised the job on LinkedIn. This means that I know both of them and they know me, so it would be relatively easy for me to contact them, ask about the job, and if it sounds interesting or promising, ask them to refer me to either the hiring manager or a human resources person—and should they decide to refer me for the job, all they have to do is provide the URL to my LinkedIn profile! It's a built-in way to take advantage of the connections you have made.

Facebook, Again

According to the *Social Times*, 18.4 million Americans say they got their current job through Facebook connections.[xlv] As I have mentioned, Facebook is an excellent way to build a professional profile that is your online advertisement. It is also an excellent way to *find a job* using a variety of methods. To take advantage of this enormous platform, many companies are building Facebook add-ons ("apps," or "applications") that make it easy to connect job seekers with companies looking to hire. I have listed some of these useful apps below along with short reviews of them, but as you look for the job or career that is right for you, your should strongly consider adding Facebook to the tools that you use to connect you with your dream job.

It is a natural evolution for Facebook to turn social networking connections into business and job networking connections. *Business Insider* columnist Heather R. Huhman listed several Facebook job apps in her article, "Job Searching On Facebook: There Are Many Apps For That."[xlvi] Heather lists several of the apps that have been developed to enable Facebook users to search for jobs. Some notable apps include:

• BeKnown: An add-on app to Facebook (you can get started at apps.facebook.com/beknown), this app creates a professional profile for you based upon the job and network information you have created on Facebook, offers the ability to discreetly let your Facebook friends know that you are interested in new opportunities, and also enables your Facebook friends to offer you professional endorsements, similar to other apps or websites. What's unique to BeKnown is that it pulls jobs from Monster.com (and only from Monster.com) based upon keywords in your work experience profile. It is an automated process. So if your title is "director of new media," it will search for and present jobs with similar keywords in the job title. If you are interested in the opportunities that appear on Monster.com but want to avoid using the website, you might consider BeKnown—but know that you are not viewing jobs from the entire universe available to you, only from Monster.com.

- BranchOut: (apps.facebook.com/branchout). I wrote a lot about using BranchOut as a way to create your own professional online presence in chapter 3, but like the other examples, it is a Facebook add-on that enables you to find and apply for jobs using your Facebook friends as contacts.

- Bright: (bright.com). Bright's functions include many of those offered in other Facebook add-on apps, like creating a professional profile and inviting friends to be part of your professional network. Like BeKnown, it pulls jobs only from one source: in this case, CareerBuilder.com. Again, it's not a bad app, but when you use it, you are limiting the pool from which you search for jobs.

- Cachinko: (cachinko.com). I liked Cachinko the least because it involved the most work to create a profile and asked to access a great deal of information from my Facebook profile. Moreover, most of the jobs that it offered that "[I] will love" were simply not a good fit. I searched for "social media" along with my home zip code and the second job listed was a concierge position in a town more than thirty miles away. In her article, Heather Huhman states that "the more feedback you give the app ('less jobs like this' or 'more jobs like this'), the more it learns about you and gives you jobs better suited to you." That's great, but with so many competing apps out there, I don't have the time to train an app to get smart about my career preferences when there are other, better apps to use.

Finally, after I installed the app for the purposes of researching this book, it spammed my Facebook friends, posting a status update on my page, which was displayed on theirs: "I just installed Cachinko! Check it out!" This irritated me and knocked this off the list.

• Jobs4Me: (jobsformeapp.com). This app is targeted to college students and enables users to "view and apply to high quality postings targeted directly to your university, receive automatic notifications of new job postings tailored to meet your preferences and employment history, share and discuss jobs offers with your college peers." The app's drawback is that it pulls jobs exclusively from college job boards and nowhere else. It sounds great if you are graduating from college and looking for entry-level opportunities, but if you are further along in your career, it's not for you.

It's Old-School, but It Works: Email

Email is the oldest of the old-school ways to get job information, but is one of the best-kept secrets. A must-have in your job search in the communications field is Ned Lundquist's JOTW, or emailed "Jobs of the Week." While the delivery is certainly not glamorous (it's a text-based email sent out via a listserv), Ned offers anywhere from forty to seventy quality job leads per week from companies all over the world. Ned has carved out a devoted and interested following of more than 10,000 people who receive his email every Monday morning. A couple of years ago, Ned also created a website to serve as an archive of the jobs, as well: nedsjotw.com. It's free, it's informative, and it's a gold mine of information for communicators. You can sign up to receive the emails on his website. Monster.com ran its first Super Bowl ad in 1999, and Ned's site started just a couple of years after.

A good and thorough job search will help you narrow and define the opportunities that can help turn a job into a social media career. Using the same platforms that you have set up, you can find the right employer by playing detective and making good use of "best of" lists, as well as using online employee opinion resources for checking out potential employers. You have an advantage through the preparation that you have already carried out—you can make technology work for you, using RSS feeds and job aggregator sites as well as tools that you already know, like LinkedIn and Facebook.

Pulling the Trigger: Sending Your Resume

Something to note when comparing different job descriptions, which we will discuss in detail in the next chapter, is that resume submission methods vary. Some organizations would like you to email a resume along with other information like salary or references, and some would like you to create an online profile which can include either a step to upload your resume along with some contact information, filling in fields within a web page that make up your resume, or both.

The most important step in communicating your skills and experience in a way that positions you as a potential match for the employer is to *customize* each resume you send out—and save a copy of it for if and when you are called for an interview. "Spray and pray" does not work well when sending resumes. If the employer stresses project management experience, change words in your resume from "accomplished XYZ" to "managed a project consisting of the following elements." Copy as many of the verbs and words from the job description as you can, while, of course, still being truthful. It might seem obvious, but matching the words in the job description makes you a *better match* in the eyes of the person who is reading the resume.

Also remember to list your online profiles at the top of your resume, just beneath your name and address: your LinkedIn profile, blog, website, BranchOut profile, anything that is public that shows that you "get it" and have proof that you already are a good online communicator.

Finally, keep a spreadsheet or another type of list of the resumes that you send out and the companies to which you send them, along with the dates. It gets confusing when you have a lot of resumes out there, so if and when you are contacted, you want to ensure that you can quickly and easily access the resume that you customized for the organization that contacts you.

Summary

As you are well on your way to becoming a savvy social media practitioner, you'll discover that your job search can have reactive and proactive elements. You can build a set of terrific social media properties and wait for the world to discover you, but you can also get aggressive and look for job that fits you using the same social media tools that you have used to build your online presence.

Now it's now time to move on to chapter 6, "Understanding Job Roles and Responsibilities," where we will explore the next step: weeding through the job openings that come along and trying to make sense of all of the web 2.0 mumbo-jumbo job titles, roles, and responsibilities.

CHAPTER 6
UNDERSTANDING JOB ROLES AND RESPONSIBILITIES

"If you make it your goal to understand social media in the context of your current business, to experiment a little, to harness its awesome power, to make it work for you, your chances of achieving success dramatically increase."
—*Lon Safko and David K. Brake, The Social Media Bible*[xlvii]

Choosing a Role That Is Right for You

Beginning a career in social media, while exciting, can also be confusing. And like the quote says, you'll have to experiment a little: with interviewing, with networking, and with different jobs within the same company or with different companies. What's odd about social media is that, unlike many other more traditional careers, there are so many job titles and job descriptions that can mean so many different "experiments" that it can be wildly confusing.

Much of the uncertainty in social media roles and responsibilities is due to ambiguity or differing definitions on the part of employers; as I mentioned in chapter 1, "Making the Choice," even at a senior level, your job is to "figure it out." Figuring it out means interpreting job titles and job descriptions, and when you land the job, figuring out what you will actually be doing. When you are attempting to interpret intent through opaque job descriptions, it can be like learning another language—one that will vary from employer to employer.

Why You Need to Make Sense of This

Weeding through, investigating, and understanding the multitude of titles, roles, and responsibilities is critical because it will help you decide if you are interested in the job (read: what you will *actually* be doing) and if applying and preparing for interviews is worth your time and effort. If you are in fact interested, and proceed to do well and love the work, that will move you from having a job in social media to progressing in a career in social media. Figuring out confusing job titles is step one.

Confusing, Redundant, and Abundant Job Titles

In her blog post "You're a Social Media Whatsit?—An Overabundance of Social Media Job Titles," [xlviii] Jennifer Mattern provides a long and wonderfully confusing list of social media job titles. I love this list because it demonstrates the ambiguity and preponderance of titles, roles, and responsibilities that exist in the world of social media. She states, correctly: "We're at a point where it seems like everyone is defining these social media job titles so differently that in the end they mean little to nothing." Jennifer compiled the list from "sources including other blogs, Facebook, LinkedIn, and job search sites. Each of these jobs in some way involved the management of a company's social media use and participation."[xlix] She put a lot of research into this, and it helps reinforce that a lot of social media is "figuring it out."

There are a shocking *seventy-five* titles that Jennifer came up with in her blog post based upon her research. While I don't have the job description for each, many of them appear to be redundant: employers' interpretations of what may be the same jobs, just with different titles. Simply reading the list is mind-boggling, but below, I'll put some of the more common ones in groups and lay out some of the likely roles and responsibilities of each.

- Blogger-in-Chief
- Brand Ambassador
- Brand Promoter
- Director of Enterprise Communications
- Director of Integrated Media
- Director of PR & Social Media

- Director of Social Media
- Director of Social Media Strategy
- Digital Marketing Manager
- Digital Media Strategist
- Digital PR Consultant
- Digital/Social Media Strategist
- Ghost Blogger
- Head of Search Marketing
- Mobile Social Media Developer
- Multi-media Communications Specialist
- New Media Coordinator
- New Media Developer
- New Media Specialist
- Online Community and Social Media Czar
- Social Impact Manager
- Social Media Activist
- Social Media Advocate
- Social Media Community Manager
- Social Media Consultant
- Social Media Coordinator
- Social Media Evangelist
- Social Media Guru
- Social Media Lead
- Social Media Missionary
- Social Media Rockstar
- Social Media Strategist
- Tweeter/Ghost Tweeter
- Youth Marketing Manager

Making Sense of Social Media Job Title Babble

Since I have been in and around what is now called social media since about 1997, I'll interpret *some* of what I believe to be the roles of a select few from the original list as well as some of the core skills sets required. I could spend the rest of the book simply describing each of these jobs, so I have narrowed the original list to those titles which are confusing or redundant—and perhaps easier to understand.

Job Set #1: Analytics Manager/Head of Search Marketing/Search and Social Media Optimizer

All of these job titles say one thing to me: measurement. Measurement is one of the least-understood fields in the world of social media. Some things, such as the number of unique visitor sessions, can be very clearly measured while other things, including customer sentiment or loyalty, simply cannot be measured but are equally important. If you want to learn more about public relations measurement, I *highly* recommend buying Katie Payne's book *Measuring Public Relations*.[1] I used this book in my class at Georgetown, and in my mind, Katie is the queen of public relations measurement. Arming yourself with many of the insights that she provides in her excellent book and measurement blog (kdpaine.blogs.com) will help you in your career enormously when you are attempting to quantify what you already know about the value of using public relations and social media. It will also help you win a lot of arguments about what is and is not measureable in the world of communications.

Fast Company's December 2011 article, "A CEO's Guide To Social Media In 2012,"[li] summed up measurement and, more importantly, why it matters:

> Most companies wait too long before asking how each potential opportunity will be measured. Don't be fooled into believing that social media "listening" is the same as program measurement. Ensure your CFO understands what is being spent, why, and what the benefits are. Different

business functions, including marketing, PR, sales, and customer care, are all measured differently.

In short, know what you are going to measure *before* you undertake your social media campaign.

What You Can Measure

The beauty of having an online presence—a website, a Facebook page, a YouTube account—is that what occurs between a computer and a website is highly measurable. When you sit at your computer and do a search in Google, log on to Facebook, or look at a video on YouTube, rest assured that someone is measuring it. If the person on the analytics side of the site you are looking at is smart, they are looking at how you got there (called "referrals" when they come from search engines and other websites). When people whose job it is to analyze web traffic use a good tool like Google Analytics (a web-based program that generates statistics about vistors to a website), they become analysts who can mine the data based upon the records created when someone finds, visits, and clicks through a site. This includes facts like:

- Visitors: How many people came to your site, and how many were "unique visitors," as opposed to repeat visitors? (A "visitor" may be the same person coming to your site more than once.) How many pages did they look at while they were there? How long did they spend on the site?

- Traffic sources: This is one of my favorite statistics, because it tells me how people are finding my site. It's a report card on how I am doing based upon my promotional efforts. You can learn how many people came straight to your site, perhaps from word-of-mouth, and how many found it in a search engine, and which search terms they used to find it.

- Traffic sources can also have a dollar figure attached to them. If you are paying for promotion through channels such as Google AdWords or Facebook ads, you want to know how many people are seeing the ads and clicking through to your site. We'll discuss more about paying for online advertising in chapter 11, "A Real-World Scenario of How You Can Build a Social Media Program."

- Keywords: These are the terms that people type into a search engine, mainly Google, to find your site—and they are another great source of data. You can learn the most popular search terms that lead people to your site and include more of them in the text and meta tags that you use. It's sort of a no-brainer: if people are using a certain word to find you, make sure you use more of that particular word or term on your site.

- Popular pages: Finally, using Google Analytics, you can determine which of your pages are most frequently visited. Look at the content of these pages. Why are they popular? What did you write about on these pages? For example, as I have mentioned, when I began writing this book, I developed an accompanying blog. As I write this, the most popular page, aside from the home page, is one that contains a the post "Social Media: Things to Think About in Working for an Agency."[lii]

What You Cannot Measure

At the opposite end of the social media measurement spectrum is the complete and utter *lack* of ability to measure what is probably the most important part of your efforts: relationship building. "Social media" *is* social engagement with people, just like making friends and deepening relationships with people on an individual basis in the offline world. It's hard for many communications management professionals (presumably, your bosses) to understand, but you can't measure making a friend, taking her to a baseball game, and the resulting engagement that means a deeper relationship. In short, in many ways, you *cannot accurately measure social media engagement.*

The question will come during your career in social media: you boss will ask you, "Why are we spending all of this money to get people to 'Like' our Facebook page? There's no direct correlation to sales. What is the ROI on this social media mumbo-jumbo?"

Take a deep breath. Explain the measurement statistics that you do have, but be prepared to tell her that you simply cannot measure establishing and deepening a relationship with someone, similar to how you cannot do so in the offline world. I do have a favorite anecdote that does, in fact, tend to resonate with many social media practitioners and higher-ups. Probably you have a similar example of your own. So, when you get that question, ask a question of your own:

> **Boss:** Why are we spending so much money on social media when you can't tell me what we are getting out of it?
>
> **You:** Social media is about engagement. We are establishing and developing relationships with people who care about our organization and our issues.
>
> **Boss:** I am busy and don't have time for all of this. What does it mean?
>
> **You (ducking):** Do we have baseball season tickets to the Red Sox? Yes, right? Do we take our clients out to Red Sox games, have a couple of beers, and bond? Yes? Well, how do you measure the *relationship building* that takes place there? The camaraderie, shared stories, and enjoyment? You can't, any more than you can measure the relationships that are established in social media. There are some things that, while very important, cannot be precisely measured.
>
> **Boss:** Harrumph.

In short, social media measurement is tricky. In some ways, its outcome is precise and illuminating—for example, when mining statistics from website visits. In other ways, the interaction at the heart of social media—being social—cannot be quantified or measured.

Job Set #2: Blog Editor/Blogger/Pro Blogger/Professional Blogger/ Ghost Blogger

As you might guess, many of these jobs deal with, well, writing for and editing blogs. Just because you can write well, however, does not mean that you can write for a blog. As with many other social media jobs, you need to have solid writing skills, but you also need to know how to write for an online audience. People don't read on the Internet, *they scan*.[liii] Jakob Nielsen, the godfather of website "usability" (determining what it is that makes a website easy to use), nailed this concept all the way back in 1997.

As a result, when you blog, you have to use shorter sentences, have lots of bullet points, use graphics when possible, and provide plenty of white space. In short, approach blogging from the perspective that your reader may or may not have time to read the entire post. What are the main points that you want to get across? How will you present these points in an easy-to-read fashion?

Someone once told me that writing for the web means taking the content that you would write for print publications, cutting it in half, then cutting it in half again. While that is not a hard-and-fast rule, I encourage you to develop the skills to write for the web once and edit once, rather than writing for print and editing twice.

Warning about "Ghost Blogging"

While each job circumstance is unique, I strongly encourage you to avoid seeking jobs with titles like "ghost blogger." This means that you are writing a blog post for someone else and that person is attaching her name to the post with no attribution to you. While this is not outright plagiarism because you are presumably getting paid for it and giving your permission, social media is based upon *authenticity*: readers want to know the original thoughts and ideas of bloggers, not what someone else writes for them. Organizations that hire ghost bloggers are advertising their own lack of understanding of how blogging works. It's OK to write for someone else if you are a speechwriter because the expectation is that the president of the United States is not going to write his own speeches. That is transparent and the public's expectation is that the speechwriter will understand the thoughts and voice of the president and the president will deliver the message. A ghost blogger lurks in the shadows and often does not acknowledge her participation in developing the blog post. It's disingenuous and violates some of the basic rules of the Internet: be honest and transparent.

I don't believe for a minute that CEOs of Fortune 500 companies all write their own blog posts, but as a consultant, the advice that I have given is that if a CEO is going to blog, let her blog. In her own words. If she does not have the time, talent, or inclination, find someone else within the organization who can do it. My super-smart friend and social media A-lister Jason Falls summed up the ethics of ghost blogging in his post "The Ethics, or Lack Thereof, of Ghost Blogging"[liv] as such:

> My definition—that ghost blogging is not an honest or transparent practice—is simple because it's clear. If the author named didn't write the piece, the naming of that author is dishonest. Just because societal norms, or lack of public concern, have dumbed us into thinking it acceptable doesn't change the definition of the act.

My advice is to avoid jobs with titles like "ghost blogger" because if you get exposed as being the "man behind the curtain" like in *The Wizard of Oz*, you may ruin your own online reputation as well as that of the organization for which you work. Finally, don't forget that if you write under your own name, you are building your own brand; people can identify your good work with *you*. Writing for someone else does nothing to help publicize your own good writing skills.

Job Set #3: Client Engagement Manager, Client Services Coordinator, Content Manager—Strategic Marketing, Content Strategist, Conversation Manager, Digital Marketing Manager, Digital Media Coordinator, Digital/Social Media Strategist, Internet

Media Associate, Multi-media Communications Specialist, New Media Coordinator, Social Impact Manager, Social Media Community Manager, Social Media Coordinator, Social Media Marketer, Social Media Manager, Social Media Strategist, Youth Marketing Manager

Just reading this list could make you confused or even give you a headache (if it has not already), but the main point here is that most jobs that have the term "manager," "coordinator," "strategist," or specialist" are somewhere between entry-level and mid-level social media jobs.

Think about it: based on the words in the job descriptions, you will likely be managing and coordinating social media projects or relationships; offering your expert knowledge about an audience, the best channels to reach them, and the best tools and tactics available; or providing strategic counsel. Many of these titles mean the same thing to me: you'll be coordinating and managing the social media strategies and tactics for a set of internal or external clients.

Why Marketing Is So Important in Social Media ⸺
Since the word "marketing" appears in several of these job titles, it's worth looking at the value of marketing to social media. Having a great social media program without marketing it is the equivalent of having your beautiful home for sale and not telling anyone—especially a real estate agent! Marketing is critical to businesses' social media efforts and there are many, many different ways to achieve marketing success.

Brian Carter, author of *The Like Economy* and *Facebook Marketing*, lists "15 Facts About Social Media Every B2B [Business to Business] Marketer Should Know"[lv]—facts that demonstrate that your future employers have not only grasped the fact that social media should be an important part of their marketing mix, but are also *using it*. This demand creates career opportunities for you in social media marketing. I've culled the list to present the top five most compelling reasons to use social media in a marketing mix:

15 Facts About Social Media Every B2B Marketer Should Know

Social media should be a critical part of an organization's overall marketing mix. It's cost effective and makes sense. Here are some of Brian's more compelling points:

1. More than 86 percent of B2B [Business to Business] companies market with social media. 32 percent use it daily.
2. B2B marketers find these channels to be most effective, in order: LinkedIn (65 percent), blogging (63 percent), Twitter (53 percent); and Facebook and YouTube are tied for 4th place (47 percent).
3. More than 45 percent of B2B companies surveyed have acquired a new customer from LinkedIn. More than 43 percent from their blogs.
4. B2B marketers use social media for brand building (80 percent), thought leadership (54 percent), lead generation (47 percent), customer feedback (42 percent), and advertising (39 percent).
5. Businesses prefer, in order, webinars/podcasts (69 percent), reading corporate social media pages (62 percent), company blogs (55 percent), and searching social media sites (54 percent).

Job Set #4: Director of Enterprise Communications, Director of Integrated Media, Director of PR & Social Media, Director of Social Media, Director of Social Media Communications, Director of Social Media Strategy, Social Media CFO, Social Media Lead

This set of job titles is also a bit more straightforward, despite the different words. You will likely be in charge of human or fiscal capital: you'll manage people, budgets, and internal or external clients. These sorts of titles will likely become more appropriate as you grow your career and have achieved the sort of experience to manage people effectively, closely watch budgets for yourself and your clients, and stay on top of the latest social media trends so that you can provide effective and meaningful counsel to your clients. Many of these skills are achieved only through experience, and there is no shortcut or substitute for being in the space, doing the client work, collaborating with others, and staying up-to-date on tools and tactics that can help you or others have an effective online presence.

Job Set #5, the Weird Ones: Community Data Guerrilla, Idea Inventor, Online Community and Social Media Czar, Serial Entrepreneur, Social Media Evangelist, Social Media Guru, Social Media Missionary, Social Media Rockstar

This list is my favorite category because the job titles make me laugh out loud. They are so ambiguous and relate so little to a social media work environment that it makes me wonder how on earth the employers came up with the titles! Guerilla? Does that mean you will be crawling through the social media jungles, capturing conversations? Idea inventor? Isn't *every idea invented?* Evangelist and missionary? Will you be put on a plane and flown to some version of a social media third-world outpost in which you will feed and clothe the social media unwashed? And czar and rock star? Puh-lease. These titles are not even worth attempting to describe because they have so many different connotations.

This is not to say that you should discount a job or not investigate it if it has a strange-sounding title. I would caution you, however, that it is my experience that when an employer wants to hire a "guru" or a "czar," the roles and responsibilities of the positions will be equally poorly defined. In order to have measurable success and progress in your career, you need a clearly defined set of job responsibilities (to the extent possible in social media), a way to demonstrate that you have accomplished these responsibilities, and an established path forward: what will happen once you successfully demonstrate that you can achieve the job objectives over a sustained period of time, and meet or exceed the requirements? Will you be promoted or get a raise? Or will the employer recognize that you can do a lot with very little definition and keep piling work on you? Remember that ill-defined titles can lead to ill-defined roles. Without having the ability to map out your future and career advancement, you can get stuck in one place.

Finally, if you want to have some fun, visit "The Bullshit Job Title Generator" (bullshitjob.com). It's a quirky and fun tool that enables you to type in a few words and come up with a poorly defined, web 2.0 job title. When I visited the site, I typed in the term "social media czar" and got back "investor interactions executive." Nice.

Quick Caveat

Job titles that are highly technical in nature will probably require you to have a completely different skill set. Job titles like "app designer/ developer," and "mobile social media developer" indicate the need for knowledge of a development platform: usually a programming language. Throughout your career in social media, you will frequently interact with programmers (many of whom are now called "developers") who will build or build out the tools and platforms that you need to be successful. They have a very defined and technical skill set. There are "front-end" programmers who develop the code that people see and interact with (like HTML or CSS, "Customized Style Sheets"), and those who specialize in the "back-end," the programming that makes everything work, like AJAX, JavaScript, MySQL PHP, Python, or Query. If you are reading this book and pursuing a different track in social media—one other than a developer—it may be helpful for you to understand what these programming languages and tools are, but it's not necessary for you to know how to use them.

Working for an Agency, Where the Job Titles Make a Little More Sense

Since I have spent most of my career in social media working for online agencies, I am familiar with the general categories and names used by major online public relations, public affairs, or marketing agencies. They are, for the most part, standard. You'll find some outliers like my very first job title, "director of online business networks," but most larger agencies take a very hierarchical approach to job titles and job progression.

When you are looking to start or advance your career and turn to the agency world, you may find some of the job titles listed below. Most larger public relations or public affairs agencies like those I have worked for (APCO Worldwide and Fleishman-Hillard) tend to like to cram social media job titles into titles that already exist in the firm, despite the fact that many of the jobs you are doing are different than your colleagues who are in more traditional roles.

Standard Job Titles

- Intern. We covered this in chapter 2, "Preparing Yourself for a Career in Social Media," but expect to do low-level work.
- Project Assistant/Junior Associate/Specialist/Coordinator. These are usually entry-level jobs, your first job in the agency world, usually when you are right out of college or an internship. While each job will vary, expect to be doing a lot of "grunt work": research, copying, drafting reports, and supporting those who are more senior to you in your agency. There is usually little input into client strategy at this level and the jobs deal more with tactic execution.
- Associate/Account Manager/Account Supervisor/Manager. These jobs usually represent more responsibilities. You may still have many of the grunt-work tasks, but expect more client engagement, like memos, reports, and perhaps participation (with more senior staff) in client meetings.
- Account Executive/Senior Associate/Managing Supervisor/Senior Account Executive. These titles usually mean middle management and these individuals usually manage (with supervision) staff and client accounts and are likely be relied upon for a fair degree of strategic advice for clients and a smaller degree of business development.
- Vice President. A vice president usually manages more junior staff and provides a great deal of strategic advice to clients. Most are tasked with delivering key insights into clients' businesses and industry environments as well.

- Senior Vice President. A senior vice president will have many of the same duties as a vice president, but with more of a "senior counselor" role: more staff supervision along with more high-level thinking. The higher you go in the agency world, the more specialization you will find as well. For example, it's fairly common for someone at this level to be an issue expert: food and nutrition, social media, etc.

- Executive Director/Managing Director/Director. This person usually heads up an office. Depending upon the size of the agency, this role could be purely management (profit and loss, human resources, strategic planning), but often can include input into client work, business development, or other details.

- Partner. This is one of the highest levels to which you can rise with an agency. "Partner" usually indicates that you have a hands-on management role in the firm and share in its profitability. Many partners also do client work as well—and may also run practice group areas.

Choosing What Else You Want to Do, Too

Many of the titles described in this chapter are stand-alone, meaning that the words offer you a fairly good explanation (or not) of what you will be doing. But what if you combine it with something else? For example, if you want to work in the social media division of the Spanish-language television network Univision, you can expect to be working on their Facebook pages, iPhone app, Twitter accounts, and perhaps other online platforms. But in addition to these social media skill sets, you will need to possess a strong understanding of marketing to Hispanic cultures, and in some cases, you will also need to speak fluent Spanish.

Your job can and likely will require you to possess or develop issue expertise as well. For example, many global public relations agencies like Porter Novelli are known for their expertise in food and beverage work as well, so you could find yourself knee-deep in doing blogger outreach to the food and nutrition communities.

What's great about building a career in social media is that you will rarely focus on one area alone or one skill set; you'll often combine it with issue expertise, cultural awareness, or even a second language.

Summary

Compared to other industries like car manufacturing, social media is still in its infancy—and this is reflected in some of the vague, wacky, or shallow job titles that you will encounter. Like many things that we have covered in this book, it will be your job to "figure it out" in terms of what you will be doing in your new role in social media, as well as how, based upon some good research and intuition, you can choose a role that is right for you.

In the next chapter, I'll cover how you can make best use of the social media tools you have set up to connect you with hiring companies.

CHAPTER 7

USING SOCIAL MEDIA TO FIND THE JOBS AND BE READY FOR THE INTERVIEW

"Diligence is the mother of good fortune."
—*Miguel de Cervantes*

"Internet! Is that thing still around?"
—*Homer Simpson*

Rest assured that this is the only book that you will read in your lifetime that contains quotes at the beginning of a chapter from both Miguel de Cervantes and Homer Simpson. I wish that I could have found one quote to encapsulate the meaning of this chapter, but chose instead quotes from different "philosophers" separated by five hundred years.

The point of combining the quotes is that even though the Internet is still a relatively new phenomenon and shrouded by confusing job titles and responsibilities like we saw in chapter 5, it is still diligence and hard work that will help you get the job you want in social media.

Presuming that you have done some research on your own and sorted through the "evangelist," "ninja," "guru," and "missionary" job openings, it's time for the interview itself. People get understandably nervous walking in to a situation with so many ramifications but with so many unknowns: Will I like the job? What would I be doing on the job? What about the work environment, salary, chances for promotion? And what if I fall in love with the job and don't get it? It can be, and often is, overwhelming. In this chapter, we'll cover where social media (Internet) meets diligence in interview preparation:

- finding the jobs that are right for you;
- researching both the companies and the people with whom you will interview; and
- Using your social media skills to help you be at your best for your interview.

Resources to Help You: Recruiters/Headhunters

While you are doing your own work to create an online profile that will help you start your career, there are many people and services to help do the job-search work for you. They are often referred to as "headhunters," or recruitment firms. One quick note: I spent several years in the recruitment field and *despise* the term "headhunter." When I would meet someone new and explain what I did for a living, more often than not the person would respond, "Oh, so you're a headhunter." My snarkiness would usually come out and I would respond with something like, "Well, I am in the recruitment field, but I have never actually lived on an island, captured someone, lopped off their head, shrunken it, and put it at the top of a pole stuck in the ground." Snarky, yes. But that term bugs me. So let's go with "recruiter" or "recruitment firm."

Permanent Job Recruitment Firms

There are a relatively small number of recruitment firms for permanent *entry-level* positions, usually because these firms tend to charge the client for their services. When an employee is hired, the recruitment firm charges a fee based upon the salary accepted by the employee, and when I was in the business, the fee charged to the hiring company usually varied from 15 to 20 percent of the annual salary. So for a $30,000 salary, for our efforts to attract, screen, and offer up a candidate who was hired, we would charge between $4,500 and $6,000.

The reason why there are so few companies that recruit for permanent, entry-level positions is based upon supply and demand. There are usually plenty of resumes for entry-level positions, so employers do not need to pay for what they can do on their own.

Temporary Recruitment Firms

Temporary recruitment firms, or "temp firms" are often a great way to get your foot in the door with a company. In her article "Top 10 Tips for Finding Temp Work and Contract Gigs," Michelle Rafter points out a couple of important things to keep in mind when seeking work for a temp firm[lvi]:

- Temp firms put people on their payrolls and then send them into short-term temporary assignments that could be either part-time or full-time. Even though you are working somewhere else, the temporary agency is your employer—they administer your payroll and benefits.

- Many temp forms specialize in finding jobs for a certain type of worker. Many find administrative or secretarial work for people, while others place "temps" in social media or even warehouse jobs. One way to find a firm that is right for your skill set is to consult professional groups such as the American Staffing Association or National Association of Personnel Services. Both have searchable membership databases.

There are temp jobs that range from short term (a few days to fill in for an absent employee) to longer assignments of months at a time, and even ones that can turn into permanent jobs. Most social media jobs, however, are not those for which you can slide in a person for a few days and get the same level of productivity. It's hard to imagine taking over a blogger relations program and a Twitter feed, simply because most social media positions are constructed around building and maintaining relationships. You can't drop in a person in a position for a few days and expect her to pick up where the absent employee left off.

My experience in working for APCO Worldwide and Fleishman-Hillard was that we tended to employ the services of a temp firm when we had a position that our in-house recruiters could not successfully fill. We had pressing needs, and when our in-house staff was not able to find qualified candidates with the right skill sets, we would turn to temporary firms first.

The advantage for both employer and employee is that you get to try each other out: will the employer think that you have the ability and skills to be an effective member of their team, contributing to their social media efforts? And from your perspective: do you like the work, the culture, and the people? Temporary assignments, although they do not offer the security of a permanent job (at least initially) often offer benefits like health insurance and are a great way to take a job for a test drive. You can gain exposure to a variety of companies and employers, hone your skills, learn about different aspects of what you are trying to do, and most importantly, gain valuable job experience.

Finally, using a temp agency can reduce the job search pressure that you may feel. Usually, your only interview is with the temp agency itself. They assess your background and skills and make the decision to place you in a job. It's one interview, and from a successful interview, you get put on a list of candidates for multiple jobs that come in. It's that easy.

Things to Consider When Working for a Temporary Firm

A common complaint when I ran temp firms was that the "temps" sometimes felt that they did not receive level of respect or job responsibilities that he or she felt they deserved, or that were offered to the employees of the company. Some felt that they got "garbage work" or were undervalued. This varies wildly from one employer to the next, but it is something important to consider.

Additionally, probably the most important aspect to consider when thinking about working for a temp firm (aside from the possible lack of immediate benefits like health insurance) is that the company does not generate revenue if they don't fill a job. Their perspective is that they need to fill the job and that you may be a cog in their job-filling machine: they may oversell a job to you that is not a good fit just to gain the immediate revenue. This is a lose-lose-lose proposition with a focus on a short-term billing gain for a longer-term loss. You will be unhappy if the job is not a good fit, the employer will be unhappy, and the temp firm will end up suffering as well if there are multiple instances of inappropriate candidates placed in positions.

Another potential downside of working with a temp firm that specializes in social media is it may not be near you or offer jobs that are near you. Most temp firms that offer social media jobs tend to be in major metropolitan cities like Washington, DC and New York. So if you are younger and looking for adventure in a new city, it's a great way to go. If you want a job in social media and you live in a small town in Nebraska, your options for temp work may be somewhat limited.

There are many lists and other resources that can help you find a temporary job. I found a few that, while you still have to do some research on your own to find the right agency for you, will at least help you get off to a good start.

1. American Staffing Association (americanstaffing.net). As an association of employment firms, they offer a searchable database of firms. The downside to their site is that the major categories are somewhat broad. The category that I selected for social media jobs was the only one offered that was even close, "Information Technology," and I had to look at each staffing firm's website (and locations) to find out if they offered social media jobs. It's a start, but one that requires a lot of research on your part.

2. National Association of Personnel Services (recruitinglife.com). This site also offers a searchable database of employment firms that match people and companies for permanent and temporary jobs. Again, there was no "social media" agency category, just a broad "public relations" category and only ten firms were listed.

3. CareerBuilder.com. This well-known site that matches jobs and candidates also has a searchable database of staffing firms. The good news is that you can narrow your search by geography and it offers the largest number of search results of my three examples. Again, the downside is that based upon your search results, you need to look at each firm first to find a location near you (or where you want to work), and then comb through each agency's

website to try to figure out if they even offer jobs in social media. When I did an in-depth nationwide search, I found social media jobs in only these cities: Austin, Texas; Redmond, Kirkland, and Spokane, Washington; Wichita, Kansas; and Sacramento and San Jose, California.

Your Own Search: The Contact Happens

By this stage, you have done your research, used your Facebook and LinkedIn contacts to try to leverage existing relationships, established an online profile that demonstrates social media expertise, and narrowed your jobs using a variety of sites. You've avoided the "spray and pray" approach by customizing each resume you have sent, rather than blanketing potential employers with a generic resume. Now comes what Tom Petty said: "the waiting is the hardest part."

Based upon my experience in the employment field, there are channels that virtually guarantee that your resume will reach the person who does the initial screening. Job boards like Monster.com, CareerBuilder.com, forms within websites, and good ol' email will get your resume there. For that reason, I would discourage you from following up with something like, "Hi there, just emailing/calling/contacting you to see if you received my resume." There is a 99 percent chance that yes, the company received your resume, and if you don't hear something back within two to four weeks, you can assume that you did not make the cut.

This runs counter to the advice that others offer, but I don't see any redeeming value in follow-up just for that reason. Most companies that I have worked with don't send "thanks, but no thanks" letters or emails until after they have selected the right candidate. It's a lot easier to say "we reviewed your credentials, but have selected a candidate for the position who closely matches our needs" after they find one than "we weeded you out at the get-go." So while it's hard, you have to play the waiting game. I have yet to see a case in which a follow-up call results in a different outcome.

Your Inbox Chimes or Your Phone Rings

There are no accurate statistics on how many people get contacted based upon resumes they sent, but if you have carried out many of the steps listed in prior chapters, there is a good chance that you will be contacted for an interview, especially if you made the right contacts, sent customized resumes, and gave it time, effort, and most importantly, patience. It may not happen overnight, but it will happen. Each day you look brings you closer to the day when you find the job that is right for you.

Where you want to work and the organizations to which you have sent your resume will impact wait times. Things tend to move faster in the private sector than in government, and usually move faster in smaller companies than in large ones. The reason is that government is a bureaucracy (always has been and always will be) where hiring tends to move very, very slowly. Private industry and nonprofits will move faster than government, but as they say, your results may vary, depending upon the number of people who are involved in the hiring process and *their* sense of urgency and workloads. And finally, smaller organizations tend to have quicker response times simply because there are less people to weigh and review resumes.

My Foray into Government Work

After twenty years in the private sector, I found out about the opening at the Securities and Exchange Commission (the job that I currently hold) from a friend, and spoke to someone within the Commission before even filling out a form. While that is somewhat unusual, it is not unheard of. Later, to ensure that I carried out all of the steps required by the federal government for employment, I filled out an online form on the website "USA Jobs" (usajobs.gov). Instead of entering a lot of narrative-based employment experience or simply submitting a resume, I played by the government rules and filled out an online form that required "KSAs," or "Knowledge, Skills, and Abilities." The National Institutes of Health website[lvii] describes KSAs as the following:

A KSA is a statement explaining your current level of competence for specific job qualifications. KSAs are often required as a part of your application package and may also be referred to as Quality Ranking Factors, Job Elements, or Rating Factors in a job announcement. "KSA" stands for:

- Knowledge—is an organized body of information obtained through education or previous experience, e.g., biology, accounting, etc.
- Skills—is a manual, verbal, or mental trait that is directly observable, quantifiable, and measurable, e.g., typing.
- Abilities—is the aptitude to perform an observable activity which results in a product or consequence, e.g., ability to communicate orally.

Filling out the online KSAs form on an antiquated government website could try the patience of Job, but if you want a job in the federal government, it's often the only way in. There are such things as "term appointments"—job openings that can get you in the door almost immediately—but the word "term" means, well, "term." There is a beginning date and an end date. At least three of my highly qualified coworkers at the S.E.C. (who wanted to stay) fell victim to term appointments, and when their time was up, had to leave the agency. Sure, it's faster, but term appointments do not offer the job security that a permanent position in a government agency does.

When I was applying for the job at the Securities and Exchange Commission, I had the advantage of being a "friend of a friend" of the person who was looking for someone with my skill set. I dutifully filled out the online form. And waited. And waited. Start to finish, the entire process of learning of the opening, completing the online forms, interviewing and getting and accepting the offer still took five months—despite my contact with the hiring manager at the start of the process! We'll address employment in different fields like government, nonprofit, and for-profit sectors in the coming chapters, but if you are interested in working in government, expect the hiring process to take a long time.

Be Ready

Interview processes often start with a "prescreen." A prescreen is very common— almost standard—and occurs when an employer reads your information, either from profiles that you have set up online or based upon you contacting them, and calls you with a set of questions designed to expand upon the information that they have in order to get a better sense of if you are a good match for the position. Whether you are employed or not employed, you need to have in the back of your mind that your phone may ring at any time—and you have to be prepared to either answer some screening questions initially or at least remember the company to which you sent the resume and the position for which you have applied. If you are on your cell phone, not near a computer, or at a job and you don't want to tip off your employer that you are conducting a job search, it's perfectly OK to politely ask the person who calls you if you can call them back. Be aware, however, that recruiters are busy and it might be your only shot to speak with him or her for a couple of days. So be ready.

When you are contacted, go back and find the job opening as well as the information that you sent to them (resume, references, links to your online portfolio), and you will be in a better place to respond to questions. If you have time, it's also a very good idea to put your social media skills to work and have the organization's website up on your computer when you are talking to the person who is contacting you.

If you get an email from a representative from the company that you have contacted, it's even better. You have more time and a chance to pull up the relevant information that the person who contacted you already has—and you are in a better position to offer more information or answer questions.

To be at your best, you should think things through first or even ask a friend to role pay with you on how things might play out during the call. Think about some obvious questions like "Why are you interested in working for us?" or "Could you tell me more about your experience working as an intern for your last employer? What were your job responsibilities?" That's where good note-taking comes in handy: if you have the job description and a copy of your resume in front of you and have rehearsed a bit, you can give good answers to the prescreening questions that you will likely be asked based upon either the information that you have prepared or simply writing down the question to ensure that you answer it in its entirety. I am known to be a bit verbose, so sometimes I give such detailed answers to questions that by the time I finish giving the answer, I've forgotten the original question!

So What's Next? Something.

Finally, after your prescreen, *something* will happen. If you get scheduled for an interview or are told that a company representative will call you for an interview, that's great. Don't leave yourself hanging, though. At the end of the phone conversation, you should ask about next steps. You will likely have a sense of the interest level of the potential employer based upon the conversation, and you can further define this by asking some probing questions. A response from the prescreener such as "we will be in touch soon" is likely a positive sign. Conversely, if the response to your question is "well, we have to continue sorting through the resumes and will be back in touch in the coming weeks," this may not be a positive sign. And remember that the person on the other end of the phone is a human being too, and it's human nature to not want to give bad news. The prescreener will likely avoid a "you are out of the running" comment at that point, preferring to do so in another format, usually after they have hired someone and then they can mail or email you a "thanks, but no thanks" communication.

Since you have invested so much time in building your online presence, if you are contacted after not having sent a resume, don't forget to ask the recruiter or human resources person how they found you online. This will help you validate some of the hard work that you have done to build your personal brand. You might even get some feedback on your website, blog, Twitter account, LinkedIn profile, or Facebook page—most importantly, from a potential employer's perspective. Knowing how they found you is critical because it may offer insight to how other potential employers will find you.

Back to Your Online Research Skills

When you hang up the phone and the result is an in-person or phone interview with the company, you might, like Homer Simpson, say "WOO-HOO!" Deservedly so. You have survived what is in most cases a rigorous screening process. To do your best and position yourself in the best possible light, it's time to once again put your online research skills to the test.

First, make sure that you get the name or names of the people with whom you will be interviewing. Your first step should be to go online and gather as much information as you can about them. Evan Kraus of APCO Worldwide told me, "In today's world, it is almost inexcusable to not ask the person who is coordinating your interviews the names of the people you will be meeting with. Do some research on them. If someone walks into my office and says 'when I got the interview, I started following your Twitter feed and I see that these are the people that you follow and these are the kinds of things that you have been looking at,' this impresses me. But don't be too detailed because it is super creepy."[lviii] When I asked Evan about the "super creepy" part, he specified that you should avoid deeply personal comments or questions like, "I see that you have four children. How old are they?" Common sense will tell you to focus your comments or questions on work-related and not personal issues.

Christopher Barger, author of *The Social Media Strategist*, offers similar and spot-on advice on what an unprepared candidate demonstrates to a potential employer: "It telegraphs that he may similarly fail to prepare for other programs or engagements while representing you. If your candidate seems to know a whole lot about social media but hasn't bothered to do too much research about your industry . . . that's a deal-breaker."[lix]

Don't be afraid to be conversational in the interview, either. In advance of one interview that I had, I looked up the LinkedIn profile of the person with whom I was interviewing and saw that he had attended the University of Indiana. Well, the men's basketball team of my beloved alma mater, the University of Maryland, defeated Indiana for the national championship in 2002 (one of the high points of my life, but not really relevant to this book). I made a joke that, since he had seen my resume, I had hoped that he would not hold the 2002 championship against me. He laughed. This approach is not for everyone (and is not "super creepy"), but it showed that (a) I have a sense of humor, and (b) I had done my research on him. In short, it helped break down some of the initial interview barriers or formality that almost always exist. This doesn't work for everyone, but if you have a sense of humor and are calm at the time, it's a good approach.

It's not just a LinkedIn profile that you may find regarding a potential employer, especially if the person with whom you are interviewing works in the social media field. He or she will have an online footprint. You will likely find a Twitter account, perhaps blog posts, online articles, or opinion pieces, and maybe even a publicly facing Facebook profile page. There are different strategies that you can employ for each of these to help connect with the person with whom you are interviewing.

Using Twitter as a Research Tool

Twitter is a gold mine of information and a window into how a person thinks, provided that the account is somewhat up to date. Unless the account is locked down (a rarity for social media practitioners), follow that person on Twitter. See who she follows, who follows her, and what she has re-tweeted as well as what she has tweeted. This will offer you valuable insight into what she thinks is important.

Do your homework. For example, if the person with whom you are going to interview follows the *Fast Company* Twitter account (@fastcompany), read a few of the articles that she references.

If you want to take an additional research step (I recommend it), *Fast Company* provided an annual list of people whom they believe to be most creative in their fields in 2011. Check out the list: (twitter.com/#!/FastCompany/most-creative-people-2011). Follow the people on the list. Read what they write. Make notes of things that you could casually drop into the conversation, mirroring what your potential boss may be reading or thinking. Try using something like, "I was reading one of Jesse Thorn's tweets the other day [@JesseThorn] and noticed although he's pretty snarky and funny, he recently provided a list of podcasts that he listens to.[lx] It's an interesting list. And did you know that he is a bailiff on his podcast, *Judge John Hodgman*? The show is hilarious."

Why Twitter Research is a No-Brainer

With just twenty minutes of research and maybe listening to a podcast or two, you have proven that you (a) pay attention to your prospective employer's social media preferences (in a subtle fashion—no "creepiness") and (b) follow not only tweets, but also influential blogs as well as podcasts. And again, you may even try to introduce a bit of humor by referring to Jesse's snarkiness (but don't force it—be humorous if it comes naturally to you or if the situation seems right). So in that precious thirty seconds, you can connect with a future boss, show that you have research skills, and demonstrate your social media savvy. You have mixed in research, practical experience, and a demonstration that you consume social media in the form of tweets, blog posts, and podcasts. These are on-the-job, real-life skills that employers value, and you have "walked the walk subtly and professionally."

Read Your Interviewer's Website or Blog

When you look up information on a person with whom you will be interviewing, especially in the social media field, you will often find a blog or personal website. This is a gold mine for determining what your potential boss thinks or feels. My own personal blog/website, *The Intersection of Online and Offline* (intersectionofonlineandoffline.com) is a virtual window into my thoughts.

In addition to social media and technology, you'll find that my communications also have some snark to them. I am active in a few charities and have blogged about them extensively. I have an entire list of articles that I have authored outside of the blog (as a freelance writer) and there is a list of podcasts which I have hosted or contributed to, as well as the audio of when I was an in-studio guest on a Washington, DC radio station. I link to my Posterous account, which discusses other non-social media topics like parenting, my personal Twitter feed (see above), and my Flickr account (a site that offers pictures—most are of personal events). But as a job seeker, you'll also see that I have posted items from two RSS feeds: one is "Jobs in Social Media" and the other in "Jobs from PRSA" (the Public Relations Society of America).

In short, if you were to interview with me and found some of my social media properties, you could learn a lot about me and be better prepared for your interview.

Another No-Brainer: LinkedIn

The LinkedIn profile of your interviewer is another tremendous potential source of information. Check and see, first and foremost, if you are connected to this individual—somehow, even via several "degrees." In chapter 5, "Using Social Media to Land the Right Interview for the Right Job," I noted that you can sometimes find out about potential jobs through LinkedIn, so if you are linked to someone who works closely with the hiring manager, you already have a connection. Most social media practitioners have a publicly accessible, robust profile that lists employers, groups, interests and associations, connections, endorsements, and sometimes tweets (my profile lists all of these).

See whom this person is connected to, whom her former employers are, and how long she has worked at the company at which you are interviewing, as well as other items that are available on a complete LinkedIn profile. One note of caution: I usually do not (and do not recommend) sending a LinkedIn connection request *prior* to an interview. Sure, it shows that you are doing your research, but I find that it borders on "creepy"—and is certainly premature.

Finally, a perfect interview cheat sheet is a LinkedIn profile saved as a PDF document. LinkedIn enables you to create a printer-friendly version that reads like a resume, and one that you can print, study, digest, and highlight prior to an interview. Bring it with you to the interview, so if you are waiting in the lobby for the individual to come get you, you can quietly and covertly review it so it is fresh in your mind.

Mark Story
Director of New Media at the U.S. Securities and Exchange Commission
mark.story123@gmail.com

Summary
Director of New Media at the Securities and Exchange Commission. Devise, develop and implement all social media "main street" and "wall street" communications using a variety of off-the-shelf and custom applications.

Specialties
Online public affairs, Internet development, client relationship management, reputation management, crisis communications, litigation communications, public relations, public affairs and grassroots

---

Experience

Director of New Media at US Securities and Exchange Commission
January 2008 - Present (4 years 1 month)
Devise, develop and implement all social media "main street" and "wall street" communications using a variety of off-the-shelf and custom applications.
1 recommendation available upon request

Adjunct Professor at University of Maryland University College
December 2010 - September 2011 (10 months)
Teach a course in the fundamentals of online and offline public relations.

Adjunct Professor at Georgetown University
September 2006 - May 2008 (1 year 9 months)
Adjunct professor and one of the founding member of the School of Continuing Studies. Designed and teach "The Intersection of Offline and Online Public Relations."
2 recommendations available upon request

Senior Vice President at Fleishman-Hillard
June 2006 - December 2007 (1 year 7 months)
Mark Story is a senior vice president at the Fleishman-Hillard Washington, D.C. office where he works with a variety of clients to design and implement effective Internet-based public affairs campaigns, start-up corporate Web sites, and online issues management projects. In addition to serving as the Interactive director of client services, Mark helps design, develop and implement online solutions for leading private companies and associations, such as Steve Case's Revolution.com, Circuit City, as well as trade associations like the World Cocoa Foundation, the Better Sleep Council and the Alliance to Save Energy.

Page1

Summary

Interviewing for jobs that are the start of your career is unnerving. As in all things, however, preparation is the antidote to nervousness. The more research you can do on the organization with which you are interviewing and its people, the better prepared you will be. Since you have already honed many of your research skills using sites like LinkedIn, it should be easier to gather information about the people with whom you will be interviewing. More preparation means better interviews and hopefully fewer butterflies in your stomach when you begin the next phase of your journey in a career in social media.

In the next chapter, we'll talk applying the work that you have done up to this point to start your career in social media, and how to continue to use your good research skills to prepare for the interview itself.

CHAPTER 8
INTERVIEWING

"Death will be a great relief. No more interviews."
—*Katherine Hepburn*

While Katherine Hepburn's quote about interviews likely deals with Hollywood press interviews, many people view job interviews with dread, as painful, near-death experiences.

I'll avoid much of the clichéd advice about "dress for success," "arrive five minutes early," etc. and leave it for other books. Rather, I will focus this chapter on presenting yourself in the best light possible as someone who not only *gets* social media but also can ask the right questions about your prospective employer's organizational culture, the work you would be doing, your role within the hierarchy, and if you will have the resources and support to be successful.

Expert Insight: Into the Mind of a Recruiter for Social Media Positions

In February 2010 on one of my blogs, *The Intersection of Online and Offline*, I interviewed Brian Batchelder, a former colleague and a senior recruiter for the global public relations firm Fleishman-Hillard.[lxi] I asked Brian a series of questions designed to help interviewees get some insight into what recruiters are thinking.

Q: I have said for a long time, "you can't teach someone to be smart." When you are looking for talent for Fleishman-Hillard, how much of a role does experience vs. interview presence—just "smarts"—make?

A: You need both. At the levels I typically recruit for (mid and senior level) you need relevant experience and have to be a culture fit. If you're smart but have never led the types of campaigns we're seeking, that won't be enough.

Q: We're in the worst economic downturn since the Great Depression. What would you say to job seekers who are looking to enter the agency side of public relations?

A: The PR agency world is ultra-competitive, even in a good economy. When you look at the largest firms, you're talking 2,000 to 3,000 people. That is tiny compared with other industries. So, you really need to do your research, talk to lots of PR agency folks, and determine what your unique, specific value proposition is. Think of agencies like a football team. There are lots of specialized roles. What niche skill can you do better than anyone else? And how will it help client X?

Q: Can you remember a candidate or two whom you interviewed and thought "this is a slam dunk?" Why? What circumstances or characteristics did this individual possess that set him/her apart?

A: This happens a few times per year with informational interviews. These folks basically have checked off all the boxes: relevant experience, great research, great questions, take notes, dress professionally, send a timely, well-crafted thank-you note, and their personality is a culture fit. They also show a strong interest in joining FH. They don't "tell me" they want to work at FH, they "show me."

A: I have written a few posts about honesty within agencies during the recruiting process. After all, agencies are a profit-driven business. Some agencies promise a lot of "work-life balance" and deliver all nighters. What are your thoughts about this?

A: The agency world is unique, and as a recruiter I almost always try to recruit people with agency experience so there will be no culture shock. You're right, it's a fast-paced environment driven by clients. You need to be flexible.

Q: Digital is the fastest-growing component of most of the top agencies. What advice would you give to a mid-level job seeker looking to latch on to an account manager role in digital?

A: Well, my take is there are two types of folks: pure digital and hybrids. If we are going to hire someone into a purely digital role, that person must demonstrate real deep knowledge and practical application of many digital channels: social media, SEO/SEM, email marketing, etc. You really can't fake it. However, a traditional PR person or journalist can really ramp up their digital skills and become a valuable hybrid (offline and online communicator). People should check out Gary Vaynerchuk's book *Crush It!* for a tutorial on how to get digital savvy.

Q: Final question: Let's say that candidates at the following levels want to work at FH. To "get their foot in the door," what advice would you give to undergrads, recent graduates, people with less than two years' experience, and mid-level people with five years' experience?

A: Undergrads: Do as many PR agency internships as possible, including one at Fleishman-Hillard. Ramp up your digital knowledge and skills. Recent graduates: Ditto.

People with less than two years' experience: Do a lot of research on our firm. Who our clients are, and what programs we lead for them. Have informational chats with our practitioners. Ask a lot of questions. Find out what specialized skills you need. If you don't have them, go out and acquire them. Ultimately, it's about defining your value proposition. What skill or niche experience could really provide value to one (or more) of our clients? Mid-level people with five years' experience: Ditto above.

Questions, Questions, Questions

Interviewing is about asking questions and exchanging information, but don't fall into the trap of going from an applicant to a supplicant. You're not begging, you are exchanging information. Although you are presumably interested in working for the group with whom you are interviewing, understand that you are checking them out as much as they are you. You will of course politely and honestly answer their questions, but you'll also need some concrete answers to your own questions in order to know if it is a fit for you. Again, I'll avoid most typical interview questions and focus on those that are unique to social media.

Let Them Start

Most of the interviews that you will go through begin with the human resources or hiring manager (or both) asking a set of questions designed to flesh out more information from your resume or online body of work. Be prepared to let them start with a set of questions designed to establish your *bona fides* and determine how much time they will spend with you. Although many people operate on tight schedules, the more time a hiring organization's staff spends with you, the better.

As part of the interview prep mentioned in chapter 6, "Using Social Media to Find the Jobs and Be Ready for the Interview," think through some of the questions that you are likely to get or the opinions that you can offer. If you read the job description carefully, have done good research, and have made good notes on what you have found, you can usually anticipate the questions you will be asked, along with some standard questions like, "So, why do you want to work here?" If you are applying for a role that would involve managing the organization's public website, expect the question, "What do you think of our website? How do you think it could be improved?"

If the position looks like a broader social media role, examine your prospective employer's entire social media presence. Look at their Twitter account(s), their Facebook profile(s), and other channels like YouTube that they use to push out information. Is their messaging consistent across the platforms, or does it appear to be customized for discrete audiences? Keep in mind that you will be employed to give solid, meaningful counsel as it applies to a business setting, so be prepared to offer insight on how social media can impact their overall organizational communications program. In short, try to look at the big picture, and perhaps even without them prompting you, demonstrate that you have paid attention, done your homework, and have valuable insights to offer.

Honest Answers

Like Cervantes whom I quoted in the last chapter (along with Homer Simpson), Shakespeare offered some solid advice about five hundred years ago when he wrote, "to thine own self be true." So when you interview, be yourself. If you have an informed opinion on why you want to work at an organization based upon your research, state your case when you answer this question. If the job description is vague or you are not sure exactly what you would be doing, say that too. Offering up answers just because they are what you think your prospective employer *wants to hear* sets you up for failure. The persona that you project in your interview will be the persona that the employer expects after you get hired. If you try to be someone whom you are not during the interview process, just think of how much energy it would take to have a different face on every day at work. Be honest and direct even if it means that you discover that the job is not for you. Again, interviews are a two-way street.

My Experience, My Honesty

This past year, I worked with an executive recruiter who sent me a job description for a high-level social media position in a Fortune 100 company. It was flattering to be considered, and after a thirty-minute prescreen phone call with the executive recruiter and a lunch with their managing partner, I was given the green light to meet with the hiring manager, the global vice president of communications.

When we met, the first question she asked me was, "So, why are you interested in working for [this company]?" My answer? "I'm not entirely sure. I have a two-and-a-half-page job description and have spent about ninety minutes with people who do not work for your company discussing the position. Sure, I have done plenty of research, but the main reason why I am here is to exchange information with you to determine if I am a fit, and if I do, in fact, want to work with your company."

My answer was a little risky and maybe a little cocky, but honest. I would rather give a forthright answer to the question than blather on about how great it would be to work for them when I really didn't have enough information. That's fake, and I think that savvy hiring managers can spot it a mile away. The approach that I took is a little risky because it could, if not phrased properly, come off as arrogant. But I would rather be honest than disingenuous.

The outcome? The hiring manager loved the answer and it changed the interview from a one-sided grilling into a conversation about how the job might be a fit for both of us. I walked away feeling good, having gotten more information from the company and the hiring executive. I could tell that my prospective boss liked my answers; she demonstrated that by telling me that she wanted to bring me to their Midwest headquarters to have a formal and final set of interviews. I ended up not taking the position, but the whole experience was positive: both my potential employer and I were honest and open with each other.

Know What They Don't Know

When you interview, also remember that most people still don't "get" social media. They know that it's important, they know it's cost effective, and they know that they need to be in the space. But my experience has been that most senior hiring managers can understand the need, but not the resources, strategy, and tactics that may be required to help you be successful. That's why it's critical to ask as many questions as you answer—and it's OK if you don't have enough information to give an answer.

For example, if you get the question "how much of a budget do you think we should have?" unless you have some real insight into what needs to be done and the resources that the company has to spend, the question is impossible to answer. It's like asking someone "how much should a car cost?" Well, it depends. It depends upon the type of car, the accessories, and other factors. No one in their right mind would give you a price for a car without determining your needs. And it is the same thing in social media. I have been asked this question before by clients when I worked for public relations agencies, and I usually said "it depends," when what I was really thinking was asking *them* "how long is a piece of string?"

My blunt method is not for everyone. Many people (most, probably) are more diplomatic than I am, so as they say in advertising, "your results may vary." Use an approach that makes you comfortable, matches your personality, and gives you the best chance for landing the job.

Some "Must-Have" Questions That You Should Ask

Go into most interviews for a career position in social media with the understanding that you are doing as much, if not more, discovery than the people who are interviewing you. This is because:

- Jobs in social media are relatively new. As you read in the foreword, most social media practitioners started in another career and transitioned into the roles that they have now.

- Many social media roles are ill defined or new, so employers aren't always sure of where to house the positions within the company (marketing, public relations, public affairs?), what the job responsibilities should and should not entail, or how social media should fit into the overall communications strategy.

- At its heart, social media is a disruptive medium. It turns on its head the traditional, top-down way of communicating. I really wish that I had a dollar for every eye-roll that I have suppressed when I hear some derivation of a fear expressed that we would lose control of "the conversation." This just in: every large organization has *already lost control of the conversation*. People are discussing widgets, securities laws, and other issues with or without you. Lon Safko and David K. Brake, in *The Social Media Bible*, describe the disruption:

[Social media] will remain a mystery to many until it becomes commonplace, in the same way that the toaster and microwave are common in your kitchen. The fact that many people will find it hard to understand what it is and how it works creates and opportunity for those who move first.[lxii]

For all of these reasons, there is a fair degree of uncertainty surrounding job roles and responsibilities in social media. You'll need to ask some probing questions that will help you determine if the potential job a good fit for you.

Question #1: What Are the Organizational Communication Objectives?

This is an essential yet often unasked or unanswered question. You can't work on, assist with, design, develop, or implement a social media program that is a part of a larger communications effort without understanding the bigger picture: the communications strategies and the target audiences.

You *must* have an idea of your prospective employer's communications objectives. If it's a corporation, do they want to use social media to raise awareness and sell more stuff, like Pizza Hut or Dell? If the potential employer is a nonprofit, would they use social media to communicate with current and potential donors to raise funds, inform members of the organization's activities, or simply try to establish a new communications channel? Or if it's government, which areas do they regulate or oversee, and how does that impact their ability to use social media—and who are their audiences? This will impact every aspect of what you do: your approach, strategies, tools, tactics, and timelines, as well as the channels that you need go through to help your prospective employer have a social media program that meets their communications needs. It's that important.

If you don't have a firm grasp on your potential employer's broader communications objectives, you can't get a full picture of how the social media piece will fit within it. And if you don't know that piece, you won't have a full understanding of your role and responsibilities. Sure, you may figure it out, but you also might flounder for a while, or worst-case scenario, pick the wrong employer, who unknowingly sets you up for failure.

My experience at the S.E.C. has taught me that in government, you may also find challenges that are unique to your employer. Where I work, we set hard-and-fast rules about what publicly traded companies can say to the investing public and when they can say it. Plus, we have rules about how we receive and respond to comments from the public. This limits how we can use social media because we can't put stringent rules on the companies that we oversee without ensuring that we follow our own rules to the letter. Many regulatory agencies like the Federal Trade Commission or the Commodity Futures Trading Commission likely face similar challenges.

Question #2: Who Are Your Target Audiences?

If knowing your prospective employer's overarching communications objectives is Rule #1, then knowing the target audiences is Rule #1a. Some audiences may be obvious based upon demographics: MTV will skew to a younger audience, one that is already active on social media ("digital natives") and may have higher expectations for products that you deliver. You'll need a fairly sophisticated approach and a set of strategies and platforms that are highly interactive. You may work at a place whose target audiences are not at all sophisticated when it comes to social media—the other end of the spectrum. For example, at one public affairs agency, a client asked me to develop a social media strategy to reach farmers. Rural farmers. Aside from buying them all mobile devices or smartphones, employing a social media communications strategy was a nonstarter. I told the client this and my bosses were not too happy. The bottom line, however, was that based upon the audience and the channels through which they were likely to consume information, social media was not the right channel to reach them. If you end up working for an agency, knowing when to work with your team to say "no" to a client is a tough sell. I have found, however, that having the guts to say "no" up front helps to avoid problems down the road after the client pays you money to achieve unachievable objectives.

Less Obvious Target Audiences

Let's say that your potential employer is a large auto parts manufacturer and *their* client is Ford Motors. No amount of Facebook "Likes" or tweets will influence those who make large-scale purchase decisions—the choice will come down to price, locations, just-in-time delivery, and a variety of other factors. Social media will have very little impact on reaching those who make multimillion-dollar purchase decisions on dashboards or vinyl covering for seats.

This does not mean, however, that social media cannot work for B-to-B companies. Using the example of the auto parts manufacturer, what if the parts they manufacture and sell to Ford or General Motors are made of materials that could potentially be considered health hazards? Plastic, lead, mercury, and a variety of other materials go into auto parts, which go into cars. As that auto parts manufacturer, the last thing that you want is to have environmental groups launching campaigns that brand you at best as a polluter, and at worst as a company that puts the health of its workers at risk. If—and only if—you have a good corporate social responsibility story to tell, your strategy might be to use social media to engage the audiences who are aware of and care about these issues through social media channels like a corporate blog, conference calls, or plant tours with influential environmental bloggers, or a Facebook page that highlights the company's efforts towards reducing their environmental footprint.

Identifying and engaging with audiences that can impact your business, however, is smart—you want to make friends and build online allies before you need them. If your employer finds itself under a public relations attack as being a polluter or worse, you will then have online allies that you can call upon to either help influence the debate by publicly supporting your environmental efforts, or staying out of the debate.

Question #3: Where Does the Social Media Function "Live" in Your Organization?

This is another critical question that will help you determine what your role will be. In the classes I taught both at Georgetown and the University of Maryland University College, I spent quite a bit of time talking about the ugliness of social media before it was called social media: turf wars. Over the years, I should have won the equivalent of a Purple Heart medal for all of the battles that I fought in turf wars.

The Nexus of Turf Wars

In the beginning, IT owned what was then not called social media. The nerds ruled. They (sort of) designed and built the websites because no one else knew how, and *maybe* took a little input and content from the marketing or communications people. Maybe. As the channel evolved, however, tension increased between the IT and communications staff. The popularity of the web and the nascent signs of social media caused communications and marketing staffs to realize that the magic was not in the technology itself, but rather in its strategic application. "Brochureware" (putting the information from your company's brochure online) was a waste and was often what IT people defined as success. As the channels became more sophisticated, however, so did the information needs of those who consumed it. Interested parties needed more than just spinning, flaming logos and stock photos.

As the turf wars escalated, communications and marketing staff made the case (or the power play) to "own" the corporate web presence. In a lot of cases, battles broke out because the IT staffs felt physical and psychic ownership of the sites. Communications people felt that IT had no clue about messaging, audiences, marketing, or many of the basic precepts of how to craft and deliver messages. And you know what? They were and still are right. Unfortunately, many of these turf wars are still being fought.

Interview Questions to Sniff Out Turf Wars

In ideal scenarios, legal, communications, and technical staffs work together to overlay social media into nearly all company activities. To get a sense of the level of interaction in your potential employer, as you are interviewing, you might want to work in the following questions:

- When was your first website launched?
- Who were the main parties responsible for launching it?
- Who "owns" the website? Or is ownership decided by collaboration between the technical and communications staffs?
- Do you have an in-house editor who reviews the content to make sure that it is "web-friendly," meaning easy to read online?
- How would you rate the collaboration among all of the parties who help produce your website and other social media channels?
- Is there a consistent look, feel, and messaging across all these channels?
- Is social media an "add on" to existing activities, or part-and-parcel to your communications activities?

These Questions Aren't for Every Situation

When you are sitting in front of a hiring manager, you may or may not get the chance to ask these sorts of questions, even though they

137

are critical to getting a sense of what you would be walking in to. If this is your first job out of college, you certainly don't want to appear arrogant. You may be limited by time (most busy hiring managers have tight schedules), or by the demeanor of the person with whom you are interviewing. If they seemed turned off by the first couple of questions, you may want to drop your line of questioning.

On the other hand, asking these sorts of questions may send a message to the hiring manager that you truly understand the dynamic of how companies operate in real life. There are turf wars. Period. And I again go back to the fact that the difference between choosing any old job or a position that will launch your career comes from choosing a job that is a good fit for you. Asking these questions and getting honest answers will help you be better informed—and will hopefully help you make the right decisions.

Question #4: What Role Does the Legal Department Play in the Process?

Speaking of turf wars and tension, it is pretty common for communications staff and the legal department to have differing opinions on what you can say publicly—and which channels you can use. As I mentioned in chapter 1, "Making the Choice," if you can't handle frustration, then social media in general and working with attorneys in particular might not be for you. Some legal staff will work with you effortlessly (as has been my experience at the S.E.C.), while others will be overly cautious, and uninformed about—and ultimately reticent to approve—online tools and tactics.

Why the Role of Legal Is So Important

Especially in an increasingly litigious society, legal departments will very often have the final say on what organizations say online, how they say it, and when they say it. No one wants to be sued, and information that you put online is forever: people will read it and consume it, and even if you take something down after you post it, we live in an age in which, when people find information that can be used against a company, they take screenshots and save them. Asking about the role of Legal is important, and the answer that you get should influence your own thinking about pursuing or ultimately accepting a job in social media.

You Won't Always Get Your Way

In my experience, lawyers are, by nature, cautious. Sometimes, being overly cautious doesn't take balance into account: the need to be part of an online debate versus the opportunity cost of *not* participating in the debate. As with IT, a natural tension exists. I can't tell you how many times, either for a client or in-house at an employer, I have pleaded the case for the use of social media to promote a stance on an issue or a product, to carry out crisis communications, or to play defense in an ongoing public relations battle. The conversations usually ended up like this:

> **Lawyer:** "We can't possibly have a Facebook/Twitter/You-Tube account. People will make comments about our issues! Bad comments!"

> **Me, (through gritted teeth):** "The debate about our issues is *already taking place*. We can choose to be part of it and engage, or choose to let people define us without participating in it. It's like a presidential debate with an empty podium and one candidate bashing the other who is not present."

> **Legal:** "No."

> **Me:** "Grrrr."

Understanding the dynamic of the prior example is important. In-house legal counsel usually rules the roost and has the final say. If your employer uses lawyers from an external law firm (as many smaller organizations do) and your bosses are the client, they can choose to accept or not accept the advice they are given. In that situation, you or your superiors may have a better chance of making the case for the use of social media because you, your coworkers, and your boss work for the company and the external law firm does not. If you are working with (or frankly, against) an internal legal counsel, there is a reason why your employer has sought the full-time services of that attorney or attorneys: there is an ongoing need for legal review and advice. They usually win.

Question #5: What Would My Responsibilities Be, and What Resources Would I Have?

This question goes back to when I mentioned that, in the agency world, many clients had "champagne taste and beer budgets." You will have some idea of the job responsibilities when you apply for the job based on the job description, and you'll learn more during the interview, but again, don't set yourself up for failure. We'll give more real-life examples of tools and tactics in chapter 11, "A Real-World Scenario of How You Can Build a Social Media Program," but know that some employers confuse *free resources* like Facebook, Twitter, blogs, or YouTube with the time and effort that it takes to build and maintain them, as well as to build an audience with whom you can engage in conversation. It's important to make sure that both you and your employer understand roles, responsibilities, reasonable outcomes, and budgets.

Questions That Demonstrate That You "Get It"

One of the best responses that you can get an in interview is "that's a great point." Since you have done your research and likely asked some good questions, you'll also have the opportunity to demonstrate that "you get it," meaning that you "get" not only social media, but how it is likely to impact both your job and the communications efforts of your potential employer. I've listed a few examples below:

Example #1: Facebook

In September 2011, Facebook mandated that individuals and businesses would soon have to change the layout, look, and feel of their Facebook pages. At first, adopting the new look and feel, called "Timeline," was optional, but eventually all users were forced to make the switch.

With a big shift like this in the social media world, if you are entrusted to manage your employer's Facebook page(s) and want to show that you "get it," you should know all about what the new layout offers (in the case of Timeline, more graphics and videos), and how it changes your responsibilities. With Timeline, you would need to know more about the graphics or multimedia support that you will need from your potential employer. Do they have video or photo capabilities in-house, or is there a need to contract out for it? And if there is no budget to contract out, do they expect you to produce the content?

Here is the new Securities and Exchange Commission Recruitment Facebook page. As you'll see, it has a more visual layout and we needed the skills of a good graphics artist to make the page look attractive.

This is an important resource-oriented question for a *free plat-form* because you could have a vibrant and nice-looking Facebook page now, but if you don't have the support or expertise to transition when the layout changes again, as it undoubtedly will, you will likely not project the online image that you want. You might even get blamed for having a bland site.

Asking the question about Facebook, explaining upcoming changes, and inquiring about resources will not only project knowledge and expertise, it will help you decide if this is the sort of job that you want to take on. It shows that you understand the responsibilities and are curious to know more about the support that will be provided to the person in your role.

Not So "Dreamy"

It's also critical for employers to realize that, unlike in the movie *Field of Dreams*, if you build it, they will *not* come. You'll need to invest the time and resources to promote your page, as well as developing other social media platforms to point people to it. You'll also need to spend the time and effort to post fresh content that gives people a reason to read your updates, not "Un-like" you, and engage in dialogue that demonstrates that there is a real person behind your Facebook page who is listening, learning, and engaging.

Example #2: Twitter

Like Facebook, Twitter is free. Moreover, your future boss might think that since you communicate in 140 character bursts, it's easy to develop a significant following. Nothing could be further from the truth. Building an audience on Twitter, just like Facebook, takes time and effort. From the moment you make your Twitter account live (or even during the interview process), you need to consider and manage *your employer's expectations* about the amount of time and effort it takes to get to what she thinks is a good number of followers. Taking the following into account—and communicating that it requires time and effort to build an audience that matters—will help you project an image of a smart practitioner and presumably avoid working for a person who has unrealistic expectations.

Twitter and Interview Questions

During the course of an interview, when you are asking questions about particular platforms and the conversation turns to Twitter, it's perfectly acceptable to ask what subject matters of substance or interest you would be tweeting. Because Pizza Hut often tweets specials, sales, or new offerings, this is likely of interest to their followers. If you work for an association and are asked to tweet "remarks by the assistant general counsel on the state of technology in hearing aids," unless that's something that is of likely interest to your followers, your chances of people clicking on the link are not great. Asking you to pick up thousands of followers with tweets that appeal to a very narrow group of people is unreasonable, and your employer needs to know that while it is likely that you can use Twitter to reach your key audiences, there simply may not be a lot of people who care.

Finally, if your prospective employer has a Twitter account or you are suggesting that they launch one, consider all of the aforementioned information carefully—and make sure that you get across the point that, as with many other communications channels like radio or TV, it takes time to build a following and get people to retain your messages.

Example #3: Video

When you are considering working for a company and doing research on them, look carefully at their use of video. Your prospective employer may have a compelling and articulate story to tell and convey it well with video, they may use the channel poorly, or perhaps they do not make use of it at all.

YouTube is still the king of online video, according to a December 2011 comScore study that ranked the most-watched video sites.[lxiii] While Vevo and Vimeo are players, if you want to reach the largest audience, this is probably where your potential employer wants to be—thanks largely to the fact that Google (the predominant search engine) owns YouTube.

The White House has an excellent YouTube channel and makes good use of video. By spending time perusing the channel, you can tell that they put significant resources behind it, including writing, and video and content organization.

Managing Expectations about the Use of Video

The needs for and use of video will vary by organization, so research and ask questions like these:

- Is video the right channel to reach your potential employer's target audiences, or those of its clients?
- If they use video well, how do they do it? Do they produce the video in-house or use a contractor? If you were hired as a social media person, what role would you play in the process?

- If they use video but not particularly well, is there a reason for this? It is based upon available resources, either human or fiscal capital? Is video simply not appropriate? And if you are hired, would it fall upon you to continue what they are doing (or not doing) online, or do you have a suggestion for a different approach based upon your preinterview research?

- Finally, what constitutes success for their use of video? Is it subscribers or total videos viewed? Or could you mine their data a bit, choose their most viewed videos and ask the person with whom you are interviewing why she thinks that is the most popular video?

As the popularity of video grows, so do your potential audiences. If video works for your potential employer or some of the clients, it's critical that you know what role you will play in the process. I have found myself behind a camera more than once with no clue on what I was doing. I got the job done, but in the process realized that there were many folks who were more qualified than I to be the one behind the camera.

Example #4: The Anchor Question

The most important question that you can ask in an interview comes at the end, and should give you a sense of how you did on the interview. The question is, "What are the qualities or characteristics that you think will make an individual successful in this position?" It's a great question because you are asking how you stack up against the traits of an ideal candidate, based upon how the interview went. If the answer to this question involves qualities or skills that you do not yet possess, or a statement like, "The ideal candidate will have experience in running social media programs for a large trade association," while you are just starting out, this is a sign that you might not be right for the job—or the job is not right for you.

Summary

Interviewing, even at the most junior levels, is about determining a fit between two parties, and you are 50 percent of the equation. To help work towards a successful or at least transparent outcome, ask some probing and compelling questions about the organization's communications objectives, the role that you would play, and how the decision-making is done, as well as the resources you have available to you. Your interviewer may or may not have the time or the inclination to give you the answers you seek, but it can only help you to gather information that will help *you* be half of the match and decide if this employer is perhaps a good match for you.

In chapter 9, "Your First Job in Social Media," I will go over what you'll likely be doing and how to help make yourself stand out among your peers and turn that job into a career.

CHAPTER 9
GETTING STARTED: FIGURING IT OUT

"You can't ask for what you want unless you know what it is. A lot of people don't know what they want or they want much less than they deserve. First you have figure out what you want. Second, you have to decide that you deserve it. Third, you have to believe you can get it. And, fourth, you have to have the guts to ask for it."
—*Barbara De Angelis, author and motivational speaker*

As was the case in chapter 8, "Interviewing," congratulations are in order. Through your preparation, tenacity, research skills, and intellectual curiosity, you have landed your first job in social media. In chapter 1, "Making the Choice," my former boss, Evan Kraus of APCO Worldwide, summed it up succinctly by stating that, since 1996, his job was and still is to "figure it out." So what will you be figuring out? Just about everything.

You may note that I have taken us from the first interview to starting on a job and I skipped over things like salary negotiation. There are other books that address the finer points of interviewing and negotiation so I'll cover just a few points.

Salary Negotiation

If you have carried out the steps of becoming not only a user but also a personal practitioner and adviser for social media, you should be paid for your knowledge and experience. You deserve to be paid for what you know, even if you have gained the skills outside of a formal work environment. Determining the dollar figure of what you are worth is hard, so here are a few tips for negotiating your salary.[lxiv]

- Don't be afraid to walk away. If you are offered what you believe to be is a low salary, counter-offer. If you are stonewalled by your potential employer ("Sorry, but we can't go any higher"), WALK AWAY. Unless your potential boss offers you a performance review in a short amount of time (say, three months) with the ability to prove yourself and possibly get a salary increase, WALK AWAY (caveat: unless you are desperate). Most of the time (and it has happened to me, too), when I can't get what I know that I am worth at the beginning, but accept the job, my relationship with my employer starts off on a sour note. Your social media skills (even if you have gained them through self-study and practice) are still valid. An employer who does not or cannot recognize this will probably squeeze you dry from a financial and workload perspective.

- Beware of the "industry average." I once was a hiring manager for a national company. My star candidate wanted just a little more money and I was fighting with human resources to get her a better starting salary. The HR person said somewhat defensively, "We have done research, and we pay the industry average." My snarky response: "If we pay the 'industry average,' we are going to get average employees who produce *average* work." This was not looked upon kindly, but it's true. Any employer who says "we pay the industry average" has a shortsighted view, unless there are several concrete opportunities to increase your salary through performance bonuses. Average salary=average work product.

- Beware of the bonus. This has happened to me at about every stop in the agency world: when I negotiate on salary, I have been told "we pay bonuses!" Hey, that's great. When I worked for APCO and Fleishman-Hillard (both were owned by conglomerates while I was there, Grey Global and Omnicom, respectively), what I did not take into account is that both are publicly traded companies. Guess who gets paid first? SHAREHOLDERS. The conglomerates' job is to keep Wall Street happy. Then senior management, then midlevel management, then junior staff. And here's another little secret: most offices that operate as part of a network of agency offices that are owned by a conglomerate view each office as a profit center. So if you are in the digital part of the firm and are making money hand over fist, yet your compadres upstairs in another practice group are hemorrhaging money, you may well be penalized come bonus time. The other practice group's underperformance affects the office's profitability, and your year-end bonus can suffer. This, while not fair, is how the game is played. One more note on the mysterious bonus: if this comes up in the interview process, don't get wild-eyed. Coolly and calmly ask your potential employer to provide you with the average bonus numbers for your position and others over the last three years. Ask what impacts the bonuses. Ask which are subjective measures and which are objective measures. You'll get a much clearer picture.

• You are worth what your next employer will pay you. It sounds counterintuitive and happens only when you get a little more experience, but if a company posts a job with a listed salary, or you interview and the position pays $10,000 more than you are making, that's what you are worth. Period. Full stop. Your market worth is determined by *the market*. I am not suggesting that you jump ship for the next big paycheck, because there are many factors to consider, but more than once, I have gauged my value in the market by speaking with other potential employers. When it came time to negotiate salary, I would bring up the fact that Agency XYZ valued me at a certain salary amount. Again, there is the caveat that your own employer knows you better than does a potential employer, but when you are negotiating, don't lose sight of the fact that what you are worth is what the market will bear.

Figuring Out "Corporate Culture"—and If It Is a Fit for You

One of the main determinants of success and job happiness is how you fit into the corporate culture of your employer. Do you fit right in, or do you feel like a square peg in a round hole? Are you willing to adapt to the unwritten rules of the social atmosphere of your new employer, or does it make you uncomfortable? Many of these questions will not be answered until you start working at your new employer. It's tough, but when it comes to understanding how you will interact with colleagues within the corporate culture over the long term, interviewing is like taking a car for a ten-foot test drive and then having to purchase the car based upon very little information.

In the book *Corporate Culture*, written by John P. Kotter and James L. Haskett, they describe organizational culture as

> values that are shared by the people in a group and that tend to persist over time even when group membership changes. These notions about what is important in life can vary greatly in different companies; in some settings, people care deeply about money, in others about technological innovation or employee well-being. At this level culture can be extremely difficult to change, in part because group members are unaware of the many values that bind them together. At the more visible level, culture represents the behavior patterns or style of an organization that new employees are automatically encouraged to follow by their fellow employees. We say, for example, that people in one group have for years been 'hard workers,' those in another are 'very friendly' to strangers, and those in a third always wear very conservative clothes.[lvx]

You may get a sense of what the culture of an organization is before you begin working there, but you won't have a true sense until you spend quite a bit of time in the work environment. In order to be successful—and more importantly, to be happy—you need to figure out if the corporate culture is a fit for you. If it is a "hard working" corporate culture (as is often the case doing social media work for an agency), are you comfortable working twelve hours a day in order to be noticed and advance in your career? If it is a "friendly culture," is that one that will make you happy, making new friends at work, perhaps attending after-work events like happy hours? If you work in an "aggressive" culture, does that fit your personality? Just like employers try to size you up during the interview process, you should attempt to divine clues about the culture of an organization to see if it is a fit for you.

Most organizations will not change their culture, but they will change employees to fit what they think of as success. Again, you'll find out important clues during the interview process, but when you finally begin working in your career in social media, you'll get even more clues early and often. Pay very close attention to the clues of the corporate culture of your employer—from this basis, you can make a decision if your job in social media is a bump in the road in your job history, or a place where you can set down roots and grow.

Expert Insight from Christopher Barger, Senior Vice President of Global Programs for PN Connect and Former Head of Social Media for IBM and General Motors on Social Media and Corporate Culture

"Corporate culture and the acceptance of social media has changed a lot in the last several years.

The answer has shifted over the last few years. [In] 2004–2007, you had to have a culture that was constantly challenging itself. There was a need for open-mindedness, a lack of fear and willingness to learn from whatever was being said. Companies that were successful had cultures that were open to being successful in social.

Now, we've moved away from first mover advantage to almost a laggard mentality, almost a catch-up mentality. Corporate cultures now are less driven by the good things of social media, the openness, the willingness to learn. Now it's a fear of being behind, of 'oh, gosh that stuff is all out there, we have to get into it.'"[lxvi]

Your Employment Future within Different Types of Organizations

In a January 2012 study, "An Examination of How Social Media Is Embedded in Business Strategy and Operations," the Society for Human Resource Management (SHRM) came up with some interesting findings concerning what your career might look like working within an organization[lxvii]:

- *In which department will you end up working?* Marketing (35 percent), information technology (IT) (17 percent), human resources (14 percent) and management (corporate/senior) (14 percent) were the groups most likely to lead their organization's social media activities. Takeaway: If you end up working in marketing (communications designed to help generate revenue), you focus will probably be on raising the company's social media profile to make money. If you end up in IT, you may focus on more technical aspects of social media, rather than communications or messaging. Finally, if you end up reporting to management or senior executives, you may have more leverage in the organization when acting as their representative.

- *Who is actively using social media?* Overall, 12 percent of organizations indicated they employ at least one full-time employee, such as a social media director or officer, who is dedicated to the organization's social media efforts. Takeaway: This is an area that is ripe for growth and indicates that while many organizations dabble in social media, precious few have dedicated the manpower and human capital to develop strategies, tactics, and presumably measurement metrics.

- *What about social media strategy?* More than 28 percent of organizations have a social media strategy. Larger organizations—those with 500 to 2,499 employees (35 percent), 2,500 to 24,999 employees (38 percent), and 25,000 or more employees (54 percent), and firms with multinational locations (37 percent) were more likely to have a social media strategy than smaller firms and those with US-based operations. Takeaway: Clearly, the larger your employer is, the better chance that it will have a social media strategy, presumably developed by social media practitioners, and this means opportunities. Chances are, however, you will begin your career in a small business, defined as one that produces less than $7 million in annual revenue.[lxviii] According to the Small Business Administration, small businesses employ half of all private sector employees, have generated 65 percent of net new jobs over the past seventeen years, and hire 43 percent of high tech workers (scientists, engineers, computer programmers, and others). You may well end up in a small business with few (or no) staff dedicated to social media. This presents a tremendous opportunity for job growth as well as the opportunity to define your own job.

- *Will your work be governed by an official social media policy?* Overall, 40 percent of organizations have a formal social media policy. Smaller organizations (99 or fewer employees) were less likely to have a policy compared with organizations with 100 or more employees. Takeaway: You will probably not only have a say in developing the strategies and tactics that formulate a social media outreach program, as the in-house expert and working with others, you will likely have a seat at the table when developing an official social media policy.

If 88 percent of companies do not employ a full-time social media practitioner, this, more than any other statistic, presents a compelling opportunity for those starting a career in social media.

As I noted in chapter 1, "Making the Choice," the explosion of social media platforms will compel many companies to begin to use social media: Seventy-one percent of companies use Facebook, 59 percent use Twitter, 50 percent use blogs, 33 percent use YouTube, 33 percent use message boards, and an anticipated 43 percent of companies will employ a corporate blog in 2012. *Someone* will need to know how to use these platforms in a professional manner to help companies achieve their communications objectives. There are too many companies moving forward quickly and a dearth of professionals devoted to the practice. That professional could be you.

Your First Job in Social Media

For purposes of comparison, I have included descriptions for two jobs: one for an in-house digital division of a large, public relations agency and a one for a private sector company. We'll examine both because your career will likely take you to many different jobs and adventures—and will start with job descriptions similar to these.

Expert Advice: Kristen D. Wesley, Agency Social Media Consultant on Working for a Social Media Agency.[lxix]

Q: What advice would you give to someone who is thinking about getting their first job in social media in an agency?

A: If you are going to work in an agency, especially for your first job, you should be prepared for an extremely busy schedule, a huge rotating client list (I work in a small agency and sometimes I have up to 30 clients at a time), and long days. And in social media, it's a longer day because communications never shut down: and online news and blogs write all day long. Be prepared for thinking quickly on your feet and troubleshooting;

be confident in what you know and the experiences you have because you are going to use those as the backbone for making recommendations time and time again. You also will have to write very fast while under pressure, so make sure that you are writing clean, crisp and in the client voice, but you have to write really fast.

Some of the best things about working for an agency are working very diverse clientele (you will have client relationships in different sectors, industries and topics) and this is good if you get bored easily. And you also will probably get to work on new business too. It's extremely fun because you get to learn about new clients, all about their business and how you get to make their business and social media strategies better.

The worst part of working at an agency is long days because you get tired and you can only be so creative for so long until your brain needs a break.

Working for a Digital Division of a Large Public Relations Agency

At random, I selected a job description for an entry-level position for the largest independent (not owned by a holding company like WPP or Omnicom) public relations agency in the United States. I chose this entry-level *agency* position because it's one of the easier ways to break into the digital field. There are more jobs in agencies than in the private sector or in associations. This firm listed many job opportunities on their careers page, but I chose one whose junior-level job title, while not vague, could use some interpretation on your part—*even after you get hired*. Here are the description and required skills of what could be your first job in social media.

Job Description

The Assistant Account Executive must have excellent organizational skills and the ability to adapt to new conditions, assignments, and deadlines. S/he must possess good interpersonal and communication skills in order to work effectively with a variety of account service staff within a specific set of accounts. S/he must have solid knowledge of MS Office Suite, Excel, PowerPoint. S/he must pass a writing test and demonstrate the ability to become a strong writer. The Assistant Account Executive is expected to hold a bachelor's degree in a related field and have interest in pursing a career in public relations. Previous internship experience in the communications field is desirable.

Responsibilities:

- Traffic jobs and coordinate projects
- Prepare client status reports
- Read and identify media clips from clipping services and online resources
- Write memos to vendors
- Work with account staff on program integration, cross marketing programs and cross promoting
- Manage post website launch basic updates, making HTML revisions, graphic replacements, and link changes to sites
- Facilitate daily client communication including scheduling meetings
- Draft client status reports
- Assist with content plans, assist with visibility audit, and assist with site audit basics
- Assist account team with creating site maps
- Assist with drawing blueprints for websites using Visio

What This Means for Your First Job

Title

The job title "Assistant Account Executive" means that you will probably be starting at the bottom of the organizational totem pole.

Expect a lot of work that will be assisting your superiors, and not a lot of client interaction. Some describe this as "grunt work," but you have to start somewhere, and this is the first rung of your career advancement ladder.

Job Description

Depending upon the agency where you choose to work, your workload will vary, but descriptions like "excellent organizational skills and the ability to adapt to new conditions, assignments, and deadlines," generally means that you have to juggle a lot of competing priorities. You may have multiple bosses, will probably have multiple clients, and you will have to be able to keep track of many different projects. And guess what? If you are successful and do a good job supporting senior staff and meeting client deadlines, your reward is often *more work*. When people within an agency begin to notice that you are a shining star, believe me, they will beat a path to your door (or, as is often the case in entry-level positions, to your cubicle).

"Adapting to a new set of conditions" can also mean on a Friday evening, you have your powered down your computer, you've put on your coat, and have one foot out the door. One of your bosses will intercept you and hand you an assignment that is due by the agency "close of business." When you are working for a public relations or digital agency, "close of business" can often mean late hours. Adapting to this is one of the more difficult aspects, and I have done it many, many times, especially in my first job in social media at the then Bivings Group in the 1990s.

Job Responsibilities

While there are many responsibilities listed in the job description, none of them surprise me—these are skill sets that you should have been developing all along while preparing for your career in social media. Based upon the preceding job description, here's my thinking on what you can expect:

- *What they say: Traffic jobs and coordinate projects, facilitate daily client communication including scheduling meetings. What you can expect:* You'll need to juggle a lot of work, keep track of everything, and keep your supervisors apprised of your progress. You'll also need organizational and diplomatic skills because agencies often coordinate several internal teams like graphic designers, programmers, writers, editors, client service personnel, and quality control experts. In a busy agency, it's not easy to balance everyone's schedule and get them to the same meeting at the same time. A good thing to keep in mind is that just about every person who is involved in working for a client believes that *their project is the most important one in the agency*, and this will be reflected in their behavior. This is where diplomacy is key if the project is not at the top of that individual's list in terms of priorities. We used to call scheduling meetings with multiple people at the same time "herding cats." Well, welcome to the world of herding.

- *What they say: Draft client status reports, prepare client status reports, read and identify media clips from clipping services and online resources.* [Note that two of these job responsibilities are redundant]. *What you can expect:* When you are starting out, this is likely about the closest that you will come to client interaction. The reports that you produce for the client will be regular (most likely weekly, unless you are doing news clips) and be reviewed by a more senior staff person before they are passed on to the client. Your name will likely not be on the reports. As for producing news clips, this is a very common offering in the agency world. Digital or public relations agencies want to anticipate issues for clients, measure success, and keep clients abreast of changes that may affect their business—and they do this by measuring the quantity and quality of news coverage. It's real grunt work, but plan on starting your mornings by searching through Factiva, Google News, Custom Scoop, Radian6, or other monitoring programs, selecting news clips that you believe are relevant to the client and their issues, and preparing and sending out the reports: *early in the morning.*

While at the Securities and Exchange Commission, based upon much of what I had learned in my agency days, I created a system whereby print clips are collected, reviewed, and distributed three times daily (with the first set going out around 7:00 a.m.), television and radio clips going out once daily, and blog clips once a week. The aim of the program, especially the clips that go out early in the morning, is to help staff stay current on what is being said about us and our issues and be better prepared for anything that happens during the day. It also helps staff stay informed about the state of the securities markets—who is saying what.

- *What they say: Manage post website launch basic updates, making HTML revisions, graphic replacements, and link changes to sites; assist with content plans; assist with visibility audit, and assist with site audit basics; assist account team with creating site maps; and assist with drawing blueprints for websites using Visio. What you can expect:* As you can likely tell from the preceding description, you'll be able to get your feet wet by using some of the technical skills that you have developed through building your own websites and social media platforms. Don't expect to be doing a lot of coding; instead, plan to use a simple HTML editor like Dreamweaver or a content management system to make changes to words, pictures, or other content on their page. A "visibility audit" usually means measurement—how your website, Facebook page, Twitter account, or LinkedIn account measures up against other platforms.

- By this time, you will probably have become fluent in many of the measurement platforms. If you are to learn one—really well—I suggest becoming very good with Google Analytics. It is widely used, and according to a recent study conducted by W3 Techs, a company that does "web technology surveys," as of February 2012, more than half—55 percent—of all websites use

Google Analytics to measure their statistics.[lxx] So know Google Analytics and know it well.

While the job description for the large agency that I offered provides a picture of the type of tasks and responsibilities you may assume, you won't know—or "figure it out"—until you get there and start the job. Sure, you may be performing many of the tasks, but how much of each? Will you spend most of your day pulling down media clips, or diving into measurement or content management? You and your employer will figure this out together. Especially when working for an agency, be prepared to spend a lot of time bouncing from one project to the next and utilizing these and many other skills.

Working in a Social Media Role for a Private Corporation

It can be harder to figure out your job responsibilities in a private sector company because the company likely focuses on something besides social media. Maybe they make auto parts or provide medical services, but at some point, people within the company recognized the need for someone to manage their online presence and they hired you.

Sample Private Sector Job Listing

I selected this job description from Indeed.com because it is typical of one that you will find in a company whose focus is not on social media. It's a little vague, contains some buzzwords, and indicates that you will spend some time determining what your role is even after you are hired because they probably don't even know what they are looking for!

Job Description

[Company redacted] seeks an entry-level Social Media Coordinator to manage web department needs and social media initiatives. Ideal candidate has a passion for emerging trends in social media and technology (mobile apps, online communities, etc.). Coordinator will support a vast digital network across Twitter, Facebook, YouTube,

LinkedIn, and more. This role is for someone who lives and breathes social media and is excited to play a key role in its future.

What They Say:
Skills and Specifications:

- Knowledge of the social media/pop culture landscape, interactive, and traditional media
- Superior written and verbal communication, interpersonal, research, and reporting skills; some technical skills a plus
- Ability to engage fans and influence digital strategy
- Self-starter/multitasker, creative, and organized
- Able to stay up-to-date with social media trends and innovations
- In-depth knowledge and understanding of social media platforms and their respective participants (Facebook, LinkedIn, YouTube, Twitter, etc.) and how they can be deployed in different scenarios
- Must have strong understanding of interactive strategy, design, production, and project management as well as tactics to leverage social media
- Understanding digital products and how to apply them to clients' specific needs

What You Can Expect:
There are a few indications in this job description that are important to the person who takes this job. It's somewhat vague and indicates that the company representatives probably know that social media is important, they are just not sure how to implement it. Here's why:

- The description begins with "Ideal candidate has a passion for emerging trends in social media and technology (mobile apps, online communities, etc.)." Mobile has been around for years, although it is growing, and online communities have existed since the heyday of bulletin boards in the early 1990s. These are not exactly "emerging trends." Moreover, "coordinator will support a vast digital network across Twitter, Facebook, YouTube, LinkedIn, and more," makes me wonder if the landscape of Twitter, Facebook, YouTube, and LinkedIn is "vast," or is their presence "vast?" And what sort of job requirement is it for someone to "live and breathe social media"?

• There are several vague job requirements like "knowledge of the social media/pop culture landscape, interactive, and traditional media," "ability to engage fans and influence digital strategy," and "a strong understanding of interactive strategy, design, production, and project management as well as tactics to leverage social media." Any job description with words like "engage," "strategy," "leverage," and "tactics" is full of buzz words that perhaps indicate a company's desire to hire the right person, but offer an imprecise understanding of the social media skill sets required to prove success for the company.

What This Can Mean for You

A vague job description can be positive or negative for you when you get the job. It could mean that you can fill out the role as you see fit, or it could be a sign of some corporate confusion or dysfunction. But there is nothing like actually working in a job, day in and day out, to determine what's it's like to actually do the job and learn the organizational culture.

A positive aspect of a vague job description is that you are likely starting from a blank canvas; what you create will be new and there will be many first-ever accomplishments as part of your job. Presumably, if you are one of the first people (or the first person) to hold this position, you will have the latitude to apply the knowledge, skills, and preparation that you have amassed to this point (I have been the first person to hold my job at the then Bivings Group in the 1990s as well as at the Securities and Exchange Commission). So while the job description might be vague, it means that, as part of figuring it out, you are molding the job to fit what you think is right.

A potential negative outcome (and again, one that you need to tease out during the interview process) is the amount of support or interference that you will have in your job. Social media is still new to many companies—some embrace it, while others know that they need to be involved, but are scared of "letting go of the message." If you end up working for an organization whose management wants to be involved in all aspects of social media, you may have to do a lot of teaching and evangelizing. Or you may get the "deer in the head-lights" look from management when you talk about how social media is measurable in many ways, but true engagement is not.

Finally, if you are one of a few or perhaps the only social media practitioner in a company, you might get professionally lonely. It's fun to be surrounded by people with whom you share interests, and much of your time at work will be spent discussing common interests. You can only burn so much time at work discussing the prior day's football game, so sooner or later, you'll want to talk about social media, what you hope to accomplish, the latest trends, or the latest controversy. If your coworkers are not immersed in social media or are simply not interested, you may feel like you are on a social media island. This is not to say that you cannot make friends and have a terrific work experience, but bear in mind that during working hours, you may have very little in common with your coworkers.

More about Your Role in a Non-Agency Setting

It's surprising, but despite the explosion of social media as a communications vehicle, the majority of companies are still figuring it out. Many need to determine where the function will live in their companies, and which policies and procedures will govern its use, as well as if and when they need to hire a professional to help them navigate the challenges and opportunities presented by social media.

Summary

Some jobs, like on an automobile assembly line, are extraordinarily well defined. You show up for work on time, find your station, and add whichever part you are supposed to add to the car when it comes down the line. Social media doesn't fit this assembly-line model. It began as a personal phenomenon but has spread rapidly to companies.

Even after you go through the process of interviewing and getting hired, your job of figuring out your role and responsibilities has only begun. If you work for an agency, you'll probably be inundated with work and clients and be challenged on a constant basis. If you choose to work for a private corporation, your role will be to establish or nurture a fledging social media function. Most people don't work for Fortune 500 companies, and if you don't, you will likely be one of the 12 percent of people within small businesses tasked with defining your role, the company's direction in social media, and what we'll discuss next—how to continue to grow your career in social media.

CHAPTER 10

ADVANCING YOUR CAREER IN SOCIAL MEDIA

"I've had a lot of jobs in my life: boxer, mascot, astronaut, baby proofer, imitation Krusty, truck driver, hippie, plow driver, food critic, conceptual artist, grease salesman, carny, mayor, grifter, bodyguard for the mayor, country western manager, garbage commissioner, mountain climber, farmer, inventor, Smithers, Poochie, celebrity assistant, power plant worker, fortune cookie writer, beer baron, Kwik-E-Mart clerk, and missionary, but protecting people, that gives me the best feeling of all."
—*Homer Simpson*

Again, Homer Simpson leads off a chapter. Sure, I could work a Homer Simpson quote into about any chapter, but while your career may not have as many twists and turns as has Homer's (astronaut and beer baron?), one thing is for sure: in every job you hold, look at it not for just what it is in the moment, but how it would position you for the next step in your career.

Expert advice: David Almacy, Former White House Internet and E-Communications Director, on How to Advance Your Career[lxxi]

- The number one quality to move ahead is that social media people have to be good communicators, not just professionally, but personally as well. You have to be able to strategically think about what messages resonate, [and] how they resonate. You need to think three moves ahead. "We put out a message on this, and this is what our opponents will say." Be educated about the issues to know what the opponents will say, how we will react to what they say, and they what their likely reaction will be to what we say or do.

- Number two is to be involved in social media tools themselves. If people don't have a Twitter account, a Facebook account, or blog, if they have not used these personally, they can't use them professionally. Don't misunderstand me; this also means that if someone is a master Twitter user, that doesn't mean that they can step in and advise clients tomorrow and be conversant about it and have some authority.

- Number three is curiosity. Curiosity is something that you can't teach. You are either curious about something, or you are not. I find that my most successful people are curious about not just what happens, but why it is happening. What did we do to make sure that a campaign that we or someone else did was so successful?

Advancing in Your Career in Social Media

You cannot advance within a company without good performance, nor can you move on to another employer without having some tangible, proven success. This can be both easy and difficult in the world of social media. It's easy in that many social media statistics (presumably successes) are highly measurable. What's difficult is that those statistics may not represent what your clients or coworkers determine is success. Let's take a look at what's easy and difficult about measuring successful performance.

What's Easy

Unlike many other careers, when you start working in a social media role, you are developing a portfolio: a public and constantly evolving body of work that proves that you can "walk the walk" when it comes to understanding the field and demonstrating success. As you compile successes in your job, write them down and keep a record of the social media properties that you think demonstrate your good work. Gather links or screenshots that you think are good demonstrations of your smart thinking and good execution. Develop, update, and add to your list, for example, things like:

- A Facebook page that you built from scratch that resulted in a vibrant, active community of followers, one that you can measure this in terms of "Likes," engagement with friends, or both.

- A corporate LinkedIn profile that has led to an increase in hiring qualified candidates while lowering the cost of recruitment.

- An intranet (private website behind a firewall) or an extranet (another private site, but accessible via an ID and password outside of a corporate firewall) that created community and enabled people to share information. If it is permissible and does not violate any confidentiality agreements, take a screenshot or two to add to your portfolio. Often the internal work that you do is equally if not more important than the public-facing work.

- If you are the first person to hold the job, have had to "figure it out" and build a social media presence for an organization with little or no precedent and guidance, say so. If you have redesigned social media properties, provide the "before and after" screenshots that demonstrate how your good thinking led to success.

While you are recording these successes, remember that all of these types of accomplishments will make you a valued employee both to your current bosses as well as your next employer. Sure, you want to focus on doing well in your current job, but if you are *building a career*, you will have several jobs during that career, and at each stop on the way, you will need to demonstrate your expertise and proven successes. A portfolio proving that you have "walked the walk" is a great addition to an impressive resume.

Advance Your Career by Mapping Out Your *Own* Goals

Even though you may have a fuzzy job description such as the example that I provided in chapter 9 "Getting Started: Figuring It Out," you will base your own happiness and success upon a combination of your employer's goals and *your own goals*. As you begin to work in your social media job, you will fulfill the role as it has been described to you, but it is equally important to map out your own *realistic* professional goals. If you are meeting your own goals, you will be happier.

As I was writing this, I emphasized the word "realistic" thinking of a good example. I once had dinner with the CEO of a public affairs firm with a digital offering in Washington, and we were sizing each other up to see if we both were a professional fit (we weren't). He related a story to me of a recent college graduate who asked him, "How do I get a job like yours?" (CEO of a successful, growing public affairs firm.) My dinner mate's response? "Go work your ass off for five years, then come back and see me."

It was a terrific answer and one that reflected *reasonable* career goals. You can't be thinking about working in the boardroom unless you think first about working in the mailroom. Understand that most of the time, you will need to pay your dues by starting lower on the corporate hierarchy—then consider realistic goals to get where you want to be. I often remind myself that no matter what I have accomplished to date, I am still the same person who started off earning $14,000 a year as a cold-caller for a temporary agency. This is not to say that I think that I am in the boardroom now, but I certainly started in the mailroom.

Many of the examples that I have given in this book are based upon two potential employers for you in the social media world: digital or public relations agencies with social media practices, and other organizations that have created or developed social media roles within their company. Let's look at moving your career forward in the agency world first.

Expert Advice from Geoff Livingston, Author and Marketing Consultant on Core Skill Sets for Social Media Practitioners [lxxi]

You need to practice diplomacy. Love 'em or hate 'em, you have to get along with your coworkers. And you have to be someone that folks like to work with. I am very mindful of the way that I interact with my colleagues; how I support them—play team ball. If you perform well and are someone that people enjoy working with, your career will go through the roof. But if you perform well and you are a jerk, you may go up the ladder, but you will get stopped. People will get in your way and create roadblocks for you because they don't want to work with you.

Advancing Your Career within an Agency

Since most public relations agencies have a clear hierarchy, it's much easier to map out your own career goals: how you want to move up within the agency. As I laid out in chapter 6, "Understanding Job Roles and Responsibilities," there are rungs on the corporate ladder that indicate progress. Within an agency, you may find titles such as those that follow that represent advancement, increased responsibilities, better compensation, and other perks (I have always asked for paid parking in every agency job. Parking is expensive as heck in Washington, DC, and it's a great perk). Decide what a real perk is for you.

Agency Career Advancement Means Making Clients Happy

Expert Advice from Christopher Barger, Senior Vice President of Global Programs for PN Connect and Former Head of Social Media for IBM and General Motors, on Making Clients Happy

First, recognize what their business objectives are. Whatever you are putting together for them needs to map back to that. A really cool Facebook campaign or a really creative micro site may make you feel good or win a couple of industry awards, but if the client doesn't see how it did good things for them, you will end up with an unhappy client. You need to map back to the business objectives, which means that you need to understand what they are trying to accomplish, so [you know] how you can apply this to the framework of their social media program.

Second, you have to keep your eye on the shiny objects, so it is possible that you could give clients counsel that "Pinterest is not for you, and this is why." What they are not willing to do is to be caught off guard when their main competitor is the first on the platform, and *you* are caught off guard saying "we'll take a look at it." You have to keep an eye on what's emerging [and] where the markets are going, be proactive, get an opinion on it, do some research, and figure out if it makes sense for your client and justify it. There has to be a reason for using—or not using—a particular platform. Close to this is to be acutely aware of what's emerging and be acutely aware of what competitors are doing, especially in the social space.

Third, gone are the old days of getting hits in Mashable and BoingBoing with millions of readers. Clients are more interested in getting mentions in outlets where their customers are. For example, there are a bunch of graphic artists who hang out on Behance (behance.net), so you better be able to recognize where your client's audience truly is. A broader approach. Look at where their customers are versus the broad push of getting as much visibility as possible. It's more about coming back to niche publications, where the clients' audiences are hanging out, how to play to a smaller community that is likely to act upon something.

Finally, don't forget that it's about them, rather than about your agency. Realize that you have your clients' goals in mind, not winning an award for your agency. As a client, I have to feel that I have the clients' interest at heart. It's all about what I can do for the client.[lxxiii]

The bottom line when working for an agency is that acquiring and keeping clients happy is your number one job. How you keep clients happy will vary wildly. Over the course of your career in social media, you will encounter clients whose level of understanding and expertise vary greatly, and your challenge will be to adapt your style to the circumstances under which your clients operate.

If you are working for an agency, each client you work with will be its own animal. Different things will make them happy. Good customer service is pretty universal, but some like to be constantly informed of progress. Others want to be left alone until they are absolutely needed. Some will have a great interest in the graphic design, while others will focus more on content. What makes a client happy will vary greatly—and what you will hear at almost every agency is that you need to make each client feel as if they are the most important one you work for.

Look at How Your Clients View the Online World

Your clients' end game is also important, and you need to help them figure this out. Most clients view social media through one of the three possible lenses: using it for marketing (generating revenue), public relations (establishing and maintaining mutually beneficial relationships with important publics), or public affairs (developing relationships with elected or regulatory officials and their influencers to sway a public debate). Or all three. Each has its own potential set of tools and tactics that may help move the needle in their favor, demonstrate success, and hopefully lead to more business for you. Clients who are relatively unsophisticated will need help understanding what they want to do, and how they will accomplish success using online tools and tactics.

Remember: strategy will inform tactics. Just because there are bright and shiny online tools that are all the rage does not mean that they will match your client's communications objectives. After determining what your clients want to accomplish, give serious thought to your recommended tactics and how you will demonstrate success. Above all, make yourself an expert on all of the platforms or tactics that you recommend: you can't make a solid recommendation without an understanding of the pros and cons of a tool.

Different Clients, Different Needs

When working for an agency, you may work with a client whose goal is simply to get online and reach target audiences (a combination of strategies and tactics). Another may have some social media presences that need to be expanded (more strategies and tactics), while others may have very sophisticated programs that need "arms and legs" to help execute (tactics, with the occasional strategic suggestion—things like writing blog posts or corresponding with people via a Facebook page). You may also find yourself challenged by a client who *thinks she knows everything about social media* because she saw her daughter make five hundred friends on Facebook.

Let's look at a few of these types of clients, and some ways to make them happy.

Client Type #1: Unsophisticated Clients/Late Adopters

These sorts of situations are becoming more the exception than the rule, but you may encounter clients whose goal is simply to establish an online presence. Most companies have websites, but you may work with a new trade association or a company who has yet to take the leap into cyber space. What to do?

As I laid out in chapter 1, "Making the Choice," most good consultants will start out by first determining the client's *communications goals* and what they are attempting to accomplish. While most likely working with your supervisors, you'll want to start with a kick-off meeting—sometimes during a half-day or all-day session—to truly get to the heart of what they are trying to accomplish online. When you ask your client the question "why online?" you may often get an answer like, "We need to be online because our competitors are," but what does that truly mean? Does it indicate that the company is losing sales because of a lack of an online presence that its competitors have? Does it mean that the organization's point of view is not present in an online debate that is taking place? Or have they simply decided that it's time to be online? (Which again forces you to ask the question "why?") Without working with colleagues and your client to determine precisely what they want to accomplish online and how you will measure it, you are setting yourself up for failure. Without goals, you cannot measure success.

Client Type #2: Middle-of-the-Road Clients

These are some of the more challenging clients that I have encountered. A little knowledge about social media is a dangerous thing, and one of your main jobs may be to gently disabuse clients of the notion that they know it all. This can be a tough sell because you want to help your clients be successful, but often they will have preconceived notions—set in stone—of what they believe will constitute success in the world of social media. There are a couple of different ways to handle this, determined largely by your relationship with the client and the budget available for the project.

Bad Situation, Happy Ending. While I was working at Fleishman-Hillard, we landed an account—a trade association—whose mission was to convince Americans to carry out behavioral change that would lessen their energy bills, and in so doing, reduce the country's energy consumption. We were going to redesign their website from one that provided minimal information (mainly about the association, not about their issues) to a platform to spread the word about the importance of personal behavior as it relates to energy efficiency: actions like using energy-efficient light bulbs or lowering one's thermostat. Mass action and behavioral change could make a difference, and it was and is a noble cause. Our mission was to re-create a website (there was minimal money to promote it) that would raise awareness of their mission, issues, and organization, and collect as many email addresses as possible for future contact, while impacting behavioral changes.

With this client, there were challenges from the beginning. First, the budget was relatively small, compared to similar projects that we had taken on in the past. As I have mentioned previously in this book, they had the dreaded "champagne taste and a beer budget." In this case, it worked out because those of us who were working on the client's account had some very, very good ideas on how to help them be successful. Early on in the project, however, there were warning signs, those that are typical of "middle-of-the-road" clients who possessed *some knowledge* of social media, but in fact did not know as much as they thought. Worse yet, there were multiple "discussions" in which we had to attempt to convince them to see things from our perspective as experts in the field of social media, and consultants who had a firm idea of their communications needs, budget, and appropriate strategies and tactics to help them achieve their goals.

Our first warning sign was that virtually every member of their staff attended every meeting. I am a believer that to be successful with a large project, one needs buy-in on several different levels. But having nearly everyone on their staff in every meeting accomplished nothing—and wasted a lot of time (and billable hours) while we covered (and re-covered) issues that we thought had already been decided. There was really no one on the client side who said, "Nope, this is the direction that we are going to take. Period. Full stop." It was groupthink at its worst, and we often left these meetings feeling frustrated and somewhat helpless. Our goal was to help the client understand the goals of their campaign (they kept shifting), and then have them leave it up to us to develop the strategies and tactics that would help them achieve those goals.

Two things saved this project from disaster. First and most importantly (and I would love to name him but do not have his permission), one of the brilliant graphic designers came up with a concept that visually and technically captured the essence of how behavioral change that began on the individual level could then translate into global change: we called it the "6° Challenge." The concept was nothing short of brilliant, and this inspired our programmers to come up with a way to turn his graphics into a functioning website. There was great collaboration between the designers and the coders. More importantly, they devised a system that not only would capture opt-in email addresses (when someone voluntarily enters her email address to an organization with the expectation that she will be contacted in the future), but it also enabled people to "tell a friend" and send an email to a customized page that contained the names of everyone in their "circle."

Finally, when you entered yours and your friends' information, you could see a graphical representation of *your six degrees of influence* on the home page of the site: yours and your friends' names would rotate around the screen. Again, the concept was brilliant and once we presented it to the client, it ended all discussions about colors, concepts, and functionality. Whew.

The second thing that saved the project was subtler. I had developed a friendly relationship with one of the senior communications people of the client and this person and I happened to be at the same conference in a different state. We went to dinner one night during the conference, and due to the informality of the evening, I was able to open up a little. I told her that due to their earlier indecision and multiple meetings, they were working against themselves, burning through their budget having the same discussions over and over again. I got her attention (thank goodness she was not offended), and from that moment on, fewer people attended the meetings, there were fewer voices, and we managed to launch a highly successful campaign. We generated buzz, captured email addresses, wowed their members (remember, a trade association needs to answer to their members because the members are the ones who pay the fees that pay the bills), and had a positive experience. We still spent more billable hours on the account and had to write off time, but it was worth it.

I offer this example because it represented a "middle-of-the-road" client: one whose staff did not, in fact, know as much about social media as they thought (there was a lot of convincing and teaching on our part), that could not make a decision without multiple people having input (it was very hard to get consensus), and that worked against themselves by burning through their budget by wasting time.

When you reach the point in your career in which you encounter clients like this (and trust me, you will), even if you have a killer design like we did, expect a lot of teaching, discussion, persuasion, hand-holding, and frustration. This account had a happy ending, but not all do.

Client Type #3: Arms-and-Legs Clients

"Arms-and-legs" clients are those who have generally solid ideas and a good understanding of what they want to accomplish, in addition to the social media tools that will help them accomplish these objectives. You will most often encounter these clients in larger organizations: they have the staff to think about the issues (they are the issue experts, after all), develop the strategies, and think through the tactics that are most important. What they often lack is the staff to help them accomplish their chosen tactics. So they hire an agency to get help with "this is what we want to do, and we need your help in doing it." So your agency may end up building the web pages, or staffing the Facebook or Twitter accounts.

Advancing Your Career within a Private Company

There are many basic similarities between working for an agency and a private organization when it comes to building and advancing a career in social media. You will want to clearly define and understand your employer's communications goals and work to achieve those goals, and in the process, make them happy. If your bosses are happy, your career should be a lot easier.

Does Career Advancement Make You Happy?

While a clearly defined career advancement path exists for many agencies, it is not always the case for other employers. If you are the first person to hold a social media role within a small business (if you are one of the 12 percent of social media practitioners within private companies listed in chapter 9, "Getting Started: Figuring It Out"), will you be content to develop a social media program, maintain it, and perhaps increase it incrementally? Does career advancement mean building out the importance of the function to the degree that you need to hire additional staff? Will you perhaps get bored or lonely if you are the only person within the company who truly understands the importance of how social media is (or should be) woven into all of your employer's communications efforts? While working in-house for an organization offers less client-driven pressure, it's important to consider your next step: if you do well and are recognized for it, then what? Will you be given more resources, both in human and fiscal capital? Or will you be making the case that a modest investment in social media can pay off handsomely, meaning that you can keep working by yourself and achieving success?

Advancing Your Career by Making Your Internal Clients Happy[lxxiv]

There are no easy answers for how to sell social media in-house, and perhaps the clearest answer depends upon how much you are invested in your job, your brand, or its place in your corporate or client's communication program. Plan on a lot of deep thinking, learning, convincing, evangelizing, and teaching. At some point in their careers, however, most of my friends have hit the "social media brick wall." This has happened to me as well. We have had some successes, achieved objectives, but ultimately become frustrated because we feel that our employers *just don't get it* because their focus is on something else besides social media. This is almost a natural progression, because if your employer makes auto parts, that is their true focus, not social media. You may feel sidelined if you or your programs are not (and I hate this term) "mission critical."

Many of my friends feel that their coworkers (and more importantly, supervisors) don't understand where social media fits into the organization's overall communications plans. And then—BAM—they hit the brick wall of frustration and a lack of understanding. Here's my advice on how to work around frustration and become a better in-house social media practitioner.

Lessening the Impact of the Brick Wall

Like any good social media program, your first task is to listen— internally. Before you tip your hand too much in the direction you want to go, give a "soft sounding" to the person who can either be an ally or an obstacle in your place of employment. Determine what her objections are likely to be and think carefully about how to refute them. But like a good lawyer, when you are building your case, think carefully about the evidence you will present and a likely reaction to it from people who matter in the process.

Internal listening and "soft soundings" are critical. To the extent that you can, listen to those who are important to your clients or your organization, and find out what they are interested in and from where they get their information.

When and where possible (and this is perhaps the most important point of all), get a commitment/dedication to social media as part-and-parcel to your organization's efforts from the most senior person you can. As we have discussed, social media has many wannabe masters: legal will want to own it, IT may well want to own it if you are building in-house tools, your communications shop will want to own it, and higher-ups may want to parachute in at the last minute and offer advice.

All of this means that there will be some refereeing that needs to take place, and the more senior level commitment to your efforts you have, the better chances you have to move in the right direction. Frankly put: if you are going to get into a battle with people who want to own the social media function, find the most influential person who has your back.

Teach and Evangelize

Be a teacher first and an evangelist second. My experience has been that the more senior people in the organization are, the more removed they are from understanding how you can augment, extend, and improve your organization's communications efforts through a good social media program. These executives are focused on selling more widgets, not on expanding social media. You have an opportunity to point out that personal and business social media accounts have different objectives, purposes, and desired outcomes. This may not always work, but if you find a generational gap, you have the opportunity to have what we used to euphemistically call a "teaching moment." When you are teaching, remember to use benefit-oriented statements and language that people will understand. When you introduce or explain Twitter, an explanation of "it's a microblogging platform with a 140 character limit" will ultimately result in a glazed-over look, especially if you are dealing with a knowledge or generation gap. An easier-to-understand statement is something like: "Twitter is a place online where people can follow us and hear what we have to say. And we can link back to our website, drawing more traffic. Plus, it's free."

The Dreaded Eye Roll

Know thine enemy. You know it's coming. You have seen it. Higher-ups who are either afraid to try or expand a social media effort, don't understand it, or are just plain obstructionist are going to ask, "What's the ROI on this?" Suppress your instinct for the eye roll and try explaining that some things can be measured while others cannot. "Return on investment" is a vague term. What is a return? A sale? An impression? A mention in a prominent blog? A relationship? Once that is out of the way, one of the hardest conversations to have and convey meaningfully is that not everything can be measured. See chapter 1 for more advice on handling this discussion.

Summary

While this book is concerned with *starting* your career in social media, once you are there, you will want to continue to advance professionally. In addition to following prescribed goals from your employer, it is equally important to map out your own career goals: what you want to do and where you are likely to be happiest doing it. This may be within an agency or in another type of organization, but what will guide you is to figure out what success is, strategize how to achieve it and measure it, and do a lot of hand-holding, negotiating, and teaching along the way.

In chapter 11, we talk "nuts and bolts" with an example of how to build a social media program from scratch.

A REAL-WORLD SCENARIO OF HOW YOU CAN BUILD A SOCIAL MEDIA PROGRAM

"You gain strength, courage, and confidence by every
experience in which you really stop to look fear in the face.
You are able to say to yourself, 'I have lived through
this horror. I can take the next thing that comes along.'
You must do the thing you think you cannot do."
—Eleanor Roosevelt

Doing what you think you cannot do is practically an everyday occurrence in social media. You will use technologies that in years past did not even exist, and you will reach people in new, interesting, and meaningful ways. And your job will change from what you think you could not do to what is commonplace. It might not be "horror," as Eleanor Roosevelt described it, but there are days that we euphemistically call "challenging."

My own "I didn't think I could do this" has happened working in small agencies, large agencies, in running my own consulting company (I am my favorite boss, by the way), working for a large government organization, and teaching at the graduate school level. My experience in social media has been based upon both book learning and practical experience. My years in the field have taught me many lessons and made me a better thinker.

Since I began in what was "online" in the 1990s, I have built, tinkered with, or enhanced probably more than a hundred social media programs. I am using the term "social media" broadly, because when I began in the late 1990s, what I did was not called social media, it was called websites. Then digital. And intranets. And extranets.

The purpose of this book is to offer *practical advice* on starting and advancing a career in social media. "Practical advice," for me, means giving real-life examples of what to expect and what you might do in a situation. So in this chapter, I am going to invent a fictitious client and lay out some of the steps that, based upon my experience, I would undertake to create and manage their social media campaign. It's real-world stuff, and I hope that it serves as a template for the some of the successful steps that you will undertake in your own career. Let's get started!

The Scenario

You have been hired as the first-ever social media person in a trade association representing the manufacturers of a controversial food additive. This additive had not attracted attention for twenty years, but has recently come under fire as being a potential threat to the health of those who consume it as part of their daily diet. The jury is still out on the science; the media likes to write about a good health scare, and there have been numerous articles questioning its health effects.

The companies who manufacture it want the problem to go away because it is negatively impacting sales. Several years ago, they formed a trade association whose sole duty used to be lobbying, but which has now found itself in the role of defending both the additive and the companies from attacks from reporters, competitors, bloggers, and others. Without the right staff in place, the role of the association shifted from lobbying to communications, and has had uneven results. They have also burned through several online and offline public relations agencies in the interim, with mixed success.

Your Role

You been hired (again, congratulations) and know right from the start that even though your bosses don't really understand how social media works, they know it's important—and that they are getting killed online. Your mission is to stop the bleeding and help turn the discussion away from the additive (the best scenario), or at least to stop product deselection that negatively affects the association's members. The member companies (those who pay membership dues to the association, and in turn pay your salary) are applying more pressure because they feel under attack; their customers are asking questions, and some have even stopped using their additive altogether. At the same time, you are the first person to ever hold this role. You've got to "figure it out" (sound familiar?). The trade association has a website about itself, but that's about it.

Top Ten Steps Plus One

In the pages that follow, I have laid out the Top Ten Steps that I think will help you successfully tackle this tricky situation. The eleventh is the social media equivalent of "lather, rinse, and repeat," meaning measuring that you have done, benchmarking it against what you set out to do, and recalibrating your program.

Step #1: Get the Messaging Right—and Consistent

Many trade associations have mission statements, but since online communication is about dialogue, you will need to have clear and consistent messaging, most importantly in dealing with such a sensitive issue. You can do some digging and get a sense of the success or failure of the association's messaging to date, but you will also need to test the online messaging. Start with Google and find out what your opponents are saying. Is it consistent? Is it inaccurate? How have people responded to what you have said? How influential are the voices that criticize you or support you? Are the opinions based upon science or emotion? What are the keywords that prominent supporters and detractors are using to describe your situation?

In the beginning, especially if you don't like the idea of defending an indefensible issue, to ask your employer for their own scientific studies and professional opinions on the additive—the truth as your employer sees it. Read as much as you can because (a) you have to become an issue expert, and (b) you most likely won't want to build a visible career promoting something that can, in fact, harm people. Moreover, I strongly recommend doing your own research as part of the *interview process* because you want to know the facts about the issue *before* you make your career choice, as I laid out in chapter 5, "Using Social Media to Land the Right Interview for the Right Job."

Step #2: Figure Out Where You Stand—and Whom People Trust

Edelman, a global public relations agency, has conducted their "Edelman Trust Barometer" since 2000.[lxxv] The survey, as its name indicates, measures whom people trust among businesses, governments, individuals, and other entities.[lxxvi] Their 2012 edition indicated that among the least trusted institutions were governments and businesses, while for the fifth consecutive year, NGOs (non-governmental organizations) were revealed to be the most trusted institutions in the world. Examples of some prominent NGOs include Greenpeace, Amnesty International, Doctors Without Borders, Oxfam, and the Center for Science in the Public Interest.[lxxvii] All of the preceding NGOs engage in some form of issue advocacy. These organizations like to present their points of view on controversial issues—issues that they hope drive awareness and impact change while ultimately generating publicity and donation dollars.

Trust Deficit

This scenario of trust (or lack of trust) creates inherent problems if you find yourself in a battle with an NGO. Your trade association represents businesses, among the least trusted sources of information. If a group like Center for Science in the Public Interest (cspinet.org) comes out against your food additive, you are contesting the opinions of an NGO, among the *most* trusted sources of information. So from the start, you are in a "trust deficit."

Social Media and Trust

Social media plays a critical role in trust. When you are working on a controversial issue that has a significant online component, understand that there are many audiences and voices in the debate. Online helps fuel the fire because people have access to free blogging platforms like Tumblr and Blogger, and almost anyone can establish an online voice—and say nearly anything they want. As part of the revolution of user-generated content (regular people voicing their opinions), many of these people become trusted online voices through their own networks, perceived honesty, and online followings.

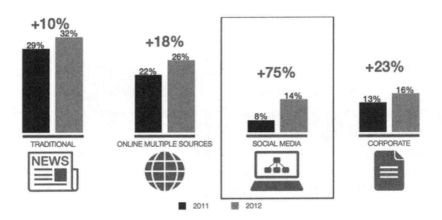

Based upon their 2011 findings, Edelman found that social media sources continued to play an important role in influencing others. The 2012 edition noted: "While traditional media sources are still the most trusted, the diversification of trusted media sources continues. In fact, social media, which consists of social networking sites, content-sharing sites, blogs, and microblogging sites, saw the biggest percentage increase (75 percent) in trust among media sources. Online multiple sources, made up of search engines and news/RSS feeds, also saw a jump of 18 percent." [lxxviii]

Trust and Your Situation

Your challenge is significant from a credibility and online perspective. You will have to begin from a position of least amount of trust, facing an opponent whose views are among the most trusted, and battle negative opinions online, where nearly three out of four people trust what they read there, especially from trust communities like mom bloggers (more on mom bloggers later). This represents a tremendous challenge, but also a tremendous opportunity.

Step #3: Planning

No one single thing will help you impact stakeholder opinions in a significant way. You'll need to plan to be both proactive and reactive when engaging on the issue and attempting to influence people to see your point of view. This includes many of the items in the steps that follow, such as:

- Determining what is reasonable to achieve based upon your association's social media budget
- Knowing how to spot and measure success
- Figuring out who your audiences are
- Developing a good monitoring system
- Deciding if—or when—to react
- Following and participating in online conversations, even if they get ugly
- Making online allies who are willing to project your point of view
- Monitoring, measuring, adjusting, and moving on

Step #4: Determining Reasonable Achievements Based on Your Budget

"Champagne taste and beer budget" applies to not only to external clients when you work for an agency, but in-house as well. Facing a problem of this magnitude, you should have a reasonable budget at your disposal. The budget may be used for things like Google or Facebook advertising, audio or video production, or perhaps hiring a social media agency to assist you. It's important to communicate that you *need financial resources* to match the challenges that you face. Limited resources will bring limited results.

The truly hard part is determining how much money to ask for. How much is enough? Tough question. Your response will take into account factors like the number of online properties that you plan to build. There are free tools like Facebook and Twitter, but serious issues need serious responses that reach the people you need to communicate with and persuade. This will likely include at least one website that attempts to project your association's point of view into the online debate.

At a minimum, I would plan on spending *at least* $75,000–$100,000 for an attractive, interactive website—and that is just the cost to build it, not host or maintain the site. By "interactive site," I mean listening and talking—your site should have moderated message boards on which you will debate or discuss the issues, in addition to other features like quizzes and outbound email. Designing and developing a good website usually means selecting a good digital agency. As you look for, analyze, and choose an agency, you should seek out one that not only builds good websites but has also done *online issue advocacy.* You can search for and find agencies in the Holmes Report agency search (holmesreport.com/research/agency-directory.aspx). There is a big difference between selling widgets and trying to change hearts and minds, so pick the agency with the best track record and expertise.

While you are planning for expenditures, don't forget some of the free platforms that can help you disseminate your messages. You will have to establish free platforms on which to post information that is favorable to your point of view: sites like Facebook, Twitter, YouTube, Flickr, and others. And while these platforms are free to join, don't forget that it costs money (staff time) to keep the content fresh and the conversation going.

Remember also that the more websites you have, the better chance you have to help "fill up" the first page on Google. Don't go cheap on websites, because again, limited expenditures will result in limited results. Planning for future expansion of the sites is critical as well, so in addition to designing, developing, and launching the site, you need to carefully think through how you are going to expand it.

Step #5: Target the Right Audiences for Your Campaign

Since you want to spend your advertising dollars wisely, you need to determine your target audiences—you don't want to take a "spray and pray" approach to the general population and hope that you will reach the right people. You'll get a sense of whom you want to reach from talking with your employer, but especially when dealing with food additives, moms are usually the ones who make the food purchase decisions—and more importantly, the conscious decisions to *avoid* purchasing a food or drink that contains certain chemicals.

The Power of the Mom Blogger

One of the most influential, well-organized, and well-connected audiences online is composed of "mom bloggers." According to Scarborough Research, mom bloggers are defined as "women who have at least one child in their household and have read or contributed to a blog in the past thirty days, make up 14 percent of all American moms (defined as women with at least one child in the household)."[lxxix] Mom bloggers are highly influential and networked, and many have established themselves as leading voices in online debates. The influence of mom bloggers has resonated even with one of the largest food franchises in the world:

"When McDonald's announced plans Tuesday to overhaul the Happy Meal—downsizing french fries and adding apples to every kids' meal—the company's top brass used every communication trick they know to get the message out: Twitter, Facebook, and more. And they didn't just invite journalists to their webcast announcing the overhaul; they also invited select bloggers—namely, mom bloggers. 'Mom bloggers are very networked and very linked-in,' Rick Wion, director of social media for McDonald's, told me. 'They spread information very, very quickly.'"[lxxx]

Consider the power of mom bloggers: the world's second largest food chain considered mom bloggers to be one of the most influential channels to publish their message about making their menus presumably more healthy for kids. This is very smart business, according to Marti Barletta, author of "Marketing to Women," who states "women are responsible for 85 percent of all consumer purchases."[lxxxi] Moms buy stuff, especially food, so getting mom bloggers on board is an essential part of many consumer and product online campaigns.

There are additional audiences to consider, such as the media and the science community, but for the purposes of this exercise, we'll focus on reaching moms, since they make the overwhelming majority of household purchase decisions and they have a powerful, networked and respected online presence.

Step #6: Advertising Your Site(s)

The world will not beat a path to your door once you build your website(s). It takes a long time to get your site into the top five or so results in search engines in organic results (how Google ranks websites without taking into account advertising). In chapter 4, "Interviewing," I laid out the importance of showing up in the first few search results in Google and the number of people who are likely to click on these links:

- Position #1: 45.46 percent of all clicks
- Position #2: 15.69 percent of all clicks
- Position #3: 10.09 percent of all clicks

Since it takes time to crawl to the top of Google organic search results, in addition to good search engine optimization, you'll most likely need to spend some money on online advertising. The two primary vehicles that I recommend are Google AdWords and Facebook ads.

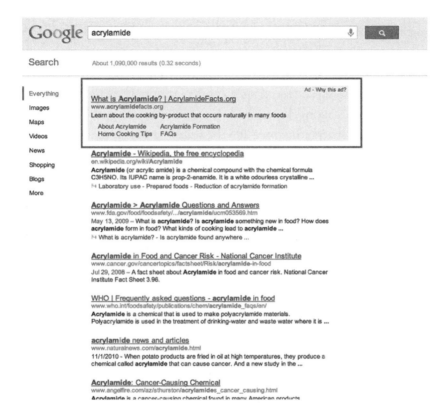

Online Advertising: Google AdWords

You need to capture people's attention at the moment of interest, when they are looking for information about your additive. To accomplish this, there are few better tools to accomplish this than Google AdWords. When people search for terms associated with your issue ("[additive] name" or "[additive] health effects"), ads with links to your sites must appear either at the top of the search results or high on the page on the righthand side. Because that's the exact moment when people are looking for information about your product or issues that accompany it. You must be there during the moment of interest.

As for budgeting, Google AdWords is somewhat complex because you need to set a baseline budget for how much you are going to spend per day or per month, and then bid on keywords. For example, you may choose 20 keywords and the most searched for term costs $4.50 per click and the lowest costs 75 cents per click. If you have a limit of $2,000 per month for clicks, assume that you are spending about $66 per day. After your $66 is exhausted, your ads will, for the most part, no longer appear (although there are ways to spread out your money).

The hard-to-predict part about budgeting for Google AdWords is that you will not have a realistic idea of how much you need to spend until you start your campaign. It may turn out that $2,000 is highly reasonable and delivers the results that you need. On the other hand, you may be "outbid" by other organizations that want their ads to appear on top of yours, so you may find yourself in a bidding war in which each one of you increases the bid-per-click on a regular basis. Determining how much to spend and how to spend it involves a lot of testing, trial and error, and refining. It's more art than science.

Online Advertising: Facebook Ads

Brian Carter, author of several books about Facebook including *The Like Economy* (briancarteryeah.com/blog), is a Facebook expert and a firm proponent of Facebook ads as an alternative to Google AdWords. Brian believes that running ads on Facebook is highly economical, much more so than on Google. Speaking specifically about this hypothetical situation, Brian told me:

"Google ads are for targeting people who are looking for something very specific. The demographic targeting is only for display ads—those go on the Google display network [AdSense sites and others], some of which are good sites but many of which are low quality. Facebook has more accurate demographic data on people, and you can target any of its ads with demographics. [For this example] . . . you can also choose to target people in a category called Parents, which has subcategories for the kids' ages. The other approach on Facebook ads is to target what people like—there are companies and TV shows that groups like moms like.

"So, first, you may not really be able to target moms effectively with Google ads. Facebook ads are also a third to a fifth the cost of Google ads, so Facebook ads are a no-brainer in this case."[lxxxii] In short, Brian is saying that you can serve up Facebook ads to moms with children who are in a certain age group, and this is a very cost-effective way to reaching your target audience.

Brian has written extensively about Facebook marketing, and he strongly advocates mixing in, if not replacing, Google AdWords with Facebook ads. As you saw, he feels that Facebook can target parents (a key audience for you), and even do based upon the age of their children. Moreover, if you are spending $2,000 on Google AdWords and Facebook ads are significantly less expensive: you could experiment, mixing $1,000 in Facebook ads and presumably drawing what would be worth $3,000 or $5,000 on Google, according to Brian's stats.

Either way, you would be wise to mix and match, perhaps with $1,000 each; see what your click-through rate (CTR) is on both platforms for a month, then adjust your expenditures based upon which is bringing you the most amount of traffic to the websites that you have set up.

With either platform, you are either reaching people at the moment of interest (when they are Googling a term related to your issue) or you are serving up ads to a demographic group that is important to your campaign and is likely to have an interest in your issue. Online advertising is a must if you want to draw traffic quickly and begin to reach important audiences.

Step #7: Listening to the Debate through a Good Monitoring System
If you are in an online debate surrounding a controversial topic, your job will move at light speed. You may leave work one day thinking everything is fine and discover that there was a massive campaign launched overnight targeting your association and member

companies and that there is a big mess waiting for you and your colleagues at the office. This is why developing and using a good monitoring system, one that serves as your "eyes and ears" online, can help you stay up-to-date on important stakeholder debates about your additive.

There are plenty of tools available, but my friend Nathan Gilliatt (nathangilliatt.com) has made it easy. Since 2006, he has been compiling a list of monitoring tools. When I say "list," this term does not do it justice. There are nearly 350 monitoring products and services on his list, all of which link to the vendors' company sites.[lxxxiii] If you are looking for the right social media monitoring and/or analysis tool, look no further.

When you select the right monitoring platform and/or service, consider: (a) if you want to use it to gather daily clips to disseminate internally, or perhaps to your member companies, (b) if you need an early warning system to alert you if an organization is planning a campaign against you (automatic and immediate email alerts for certain keywords), and (c) if you are searching for trends that will portend future issue debate changes. Knowing the information that you want to get out of the tool and what you will do with it will help you select the right one.

A word of caution: like many other social media platforms, don't be wowed by a shiny object. Flash animation or fancy charts and graphs don't matter. What does matter is (a) does the system capture the information you need from the sources that are important to you, (b) does it filter out the news and view that you don't need, (c) can you quickly adjust the tool as new issues arise, and (d) is the information easy to disseminate to other people? In short, don't pick the tool with bells and whistles, but one that meets your customized needs.

Step #8: Deciding If—or When—to React

Your monitoring program will likely bring you lots of information from multiple sources, and it's your job to weed through the sources to see which really matter. If you are playing defense (reacting to what others say), you'll need to come up with a criteria for response—when do you react to something that someone has said? What rises to the threshold of meriting a response? While this is an inexact science, I used to tell my clients that when a newspaper reporter—even one who writes for an influential publication like the *New York Times*—criticizes the president, he most often will not react since it does not meet a certain threshold for the president of the United States to come out and respond to a mere newspaper story. When a foreign leader or a presidential candidate from another party criticizes the president in a certain forum, he is more likely to issue some form of response. The reach, credibility, and potential impact of the person or organization that criticizes the president will influence his decision to respond. It's even sport in Washington to predict when, in the presidential campaign season, a sitting president will mention his opponent by name.

It's the same situation with your fictitious scenario. If you find a blog with two entries that is only updated once a month and does not seem to have much traffic, you can probably ignore the post. If you feel that you are under attack by a high-profile group or NGO with a significant reach and impact like Center for Science in the Public Interest, you will probably need to engage and respond. Your response should be carefully calibrated to the visibility and credibility of the group that criticizes you.

Don't forget that engagement does not mean posting one comment and moving on. Your hope should be to establish a running dialogue—a conversation—that demonstrates that you can politely and professionally disagree with others.

Step #9: Follow and Participate in Online Conversations, Even If They Get Ugly

As I have said many times in the book, the basis of social media is listening and conversation—and many times, patience and tolerance. Far too many organizations cannot resist the temptation to remove negative comments from an online platform. This is social media suicide because people will take screenshots of their comments, and after you have deleted them, accuse you of censoring their point of view because you don't agree with it.

Making the Best of Negative Comments

Not only is deleting comments tantamount to online reputational suicide, as we just discussed, but the comments can also give you an opportunity to strengthen your campaign. In her blog post "5 Reasons NOT to Delete Negative Reviews,"[lxxxiv] Lisa Barone notes:

1. You want the conversation to happen at home. If someone left you a scathing review on your Facebook page, you may want to consider sending them a cheese basket or something to thank you. Because, it means they were kind enough to come to you first and that there's still time to fix the relationship.

2. It's a chance to change the conversation. If someone left a negative comment or review about your company, they're giving you a chance to change the conversation and make it better.

3. You get to show off your customer service. Everyone else who stumbled upon that review/comment will care. By positively responding to a negative comment on your page, it shows everyone looking how much you care about your customers and the lengths you'll go to right a bad situation.

4. Gives you street cred. As long as you have plenty of positive reviews to counteract it, leaving a negative review on your page isn't going to hurt you. It may even provide balance and make someone feel more comfortable purchasing from you.

5. You get feedback you can act on—take the feedback people are giving you and look for ways to incorporate it into your business.

Being Open Presents the Opportunity for Dialogue

You want your association to appear to be open, honest, and transparent, and you can demonstrate this by providing platforms for people to voice their opinions, even if they run counter to yours. When someone comments on your website or Facebook page, or tweets something about your additive or your association, think of this as an opportunity to engage in dialogue. Your goal may not be to change the person's mind (especially when it comes to a highly controversial topic), but to create an online record of your response that is measured, polite, and helps demonstrate that your association is open to debating the issue and considering other points of view *when other people find the comment thread.* If you do it right, when someone posts something highly critical, you have an opportunity to look like the good guy. It may play out like this:

Commenter: Everything you guys say are lies, lies, lies. I know that you are in the pocket of big business and you don't care if [additive] is causing cancer and killing people. All you care about is the almighty dollar. You all are a bunch of shills.

Do *not* delete this comment or post. Here's your opportunity:

You: Hi, my name is Mark Story and I work for [trade association]. I am also a dad. I appreciate your comments and assure you that we take all views seriously. While I welcome your passion, I want to assure you that it is the mission of both our association and member companies to be open, honest, and transparent about [additive].

> *There are many people who disagree with your view that*
> *[additive] causes cancer. In fact, here are a couple of links*
> *to respected scientific resources that dispute claims that*
> *our product is harmful. [links here]. Please feel free to con-*
> *tinue to comment or visit our other resources [list here].*
> *Again, we welcome comments. Mark Story."*

By responding in a measured, friendly tone, you are creating an online record of your position and pointing this person (and more importantly, future readers) to alternative sources of information. You have also provided a human perspective to the issue and demonstrated that you are willing to engage in civil, polite conversations. It's hard to call your association "monsters" if you behave like concerned citizens.

Step #10: Make Online Allies Who Are Willing to Project Your Point of View

While you may have an online campaign including an informative website, a few Twitter accounts, a Facebook page, a YouTube channel, online ads that point to all of them, and other online properties that present your association's point of view, don't forget your "trust deficit." Beyond the fact that you represent businesses (low public trust), many people will view your information as biased and self-serving. For this reason, you will want to cultivate online allies—people who will add their own points of view to the online debate.

There are two ways to go about cultivating online allies and both have high risks and rewards. In my career, I have built "field teams," *paid consultants* whose job it is to proactively speak out on behalf of an association and its issues, perhaps meet with legislators and regulators, and help you push certain issues. I have also made natural allies: bloggers and other online influencers whom I convinced to adopt at least a portion of my point of view, or at a minimum, to stop criticizing me. This is the human resources equivalent of paid media vs. earned media.

Paid Staff

The good thing about paid staff is that you know they will do what you need them to do: carry your message as intended. They are getting paid to do a job. Where this becomes tricky is that (a) some organizations openly disclose their relationship with paid staff, while others do not, and (b) people who are known to be drawing a paycheck from your association will be viewed, at least initially, with some skepticism by the people whom you are trying to influence.

For your issue, you might develop a group of ten mom bloggers, scientists, nurses, and doctors to speak out on your behalf online. This may be via their own blogs, comments on third-party websites, or even interviews with the media. It will be their job to help get your message out about your additive to the right audiences and to be credible sources of information in the debate. For example, moms want to hear from moms, and medical professionals will tend to trust other medical professionals.

Having a stable of online allies—third-party voices—is critical, but transparency is more important. Not all organizations disclose their monetary relationship with their allies; it's dangerous if you portray someone to be a natural ally when she is on your payroll. It's horrible publicity, and if you get "outed," it can take away the credibility of your entire campaign.

Working Families for Wal-Mart

In 2006, Edelman, one of the nation's largest public relations firms, was heavily criticized for having several employees impersonate "average people" who appeared to be independent supporters of Wal-Mart. On October 18, 2006, CNN Money reported: "A blog praising Wal-Mart . . . called 'Wal-Marting Across America,' ostensibly created by a man and a woman traveling the country in an RV and staying in Wal-Mart parking lots, turned out to be underwritten by Working Families for Wal-Mart, a company-sponsored group organized by the Edelman public relations firm. Not cool . . . The lesson's clear. The best corporate blogs are open, honest, and authentic, according to Debbie Weil, a former journalist and Internet marketing consultant who is author of *The Corporate Blogging Book* (Penguin, 2006)."[lxxxv]

Plenty of organizations engage staff to represent their views, but if you are going to do so, be transparent about it. The Working Families for Wal-Mart debacle severely damaged the credibility of both Edelman and Wal-Mart's online advocacy efforts.

Building a Network of Natural Allies

Your issue is being fought and debated online, so your need to find other allies who can support you in the online environment, or at least stop criticizing you. Many organizations turn to influential bloggers and try to convince them of an alternative point of view: yours.

Blogger Outreach

In the agency world, we call it "pitching." Pitching means contacting a writer or blogger in the hopes that you can get him to write a story about the topic you are proposing.

While I worked at APCO and Fleishman-Hillard, we had full-time staff whose job it was to do "blogger relations": seek out, establish, and maintain good relationships with them. Trust me, this is an acquired skill. Since bloggers are easy to contact because most have the contact information online, far too many public relations people have bungled "pitches" by mistaking the ease of contact with the blogger's desire to receive a pitch that is about a topic that has nothing to do with what they write about and would not be of interest to her organization.

There is an enormous amount of controversy surrounding pitching bloggers, so you need to do it right. If you botch the pitch, you might even end up on the *Bad Pitch Blog* (badpitch.blogspot.com), a very popular site where frustrated bloggers post the pitches that they have received that they think are off target or just plain stupid. Establishing good relationships with bloggers is straightforward, but you need to put in your homework first so you don't get burned.

Tips for Good Blogger Pitching

1. Lurk first. Before approaching a blogger, read her blog posts, especially about your issue. Read the back-and-forth in the comments section of her blog. In short, get smart—very smart—about her feelings on the issue. Know her views, allies, and writing style.

2. Follow her rules. Many good and popular bloggers are now adding "How to Pitch Me" sections to their blogs. If it's there, follow the rules. Jason Falls has "How to Pitch Social Media Explorer" (his main blog) linked to from the home page.[lxxxvi] He lists seven rules, but rule number one is "We write about social media, public relations, marketing, and advertising. Sometimes we touch on how technology effects those worlds. If it's not in those categories, don't pitch us." Follow the rules and you will have a much better chance of getting heard.

3. Show you have done your homework. When you make the first contact (likely via email), show the blogger that you have read his blog and why you think connecting might be a good idea. Something like "Dear Chris, I'm Mark Story and I am with the [trade association for additive]. I have spent quite a bit of time on your blog and know that you are interested in and write about the health effects of [additive]. I'd like to thank you for adding your voice to the online discussion about it. I am writing because I am wondering if you would be interested in having a conversation with us about [additive]. Clearly, I represent the industry, but I have some viewpoints that may be of interest to you and your readers. Would you be interested in talking at some point, even via email?"

4. Understand that everything that you communicate may—and sometimes will—be published. Every word in your email should be written as if you were putting it above the fold in the *New York Times*. Many bloggers, even when considering pitches from agencies or other organizations, will publish the entire

transcript of conversations, so don't say anything that you will regret.

5. If possible, try to get a phone conversation. It's a lot easier to have a back-and-forth or exchange of ideas via the telephone than in writing. It also helps to build relationships and avoid misunderstandings. Again, understand that the blogger may or may not trust you, so assume that she is recording the conversation or at least transcribing every word you say. Be careful.

6. Finally, understand that you are not going to convert everyone to your point of view. In fact, if you are operating in the "trust deficit" we discussed before, know that you will most likely *not convert* most of the bloggers whom you are pitching. Trying to influence the online debate, however, means influencing the influencers— and in our case, it's the bloggers. You've got to try.

Step #11: Monitoring, Measuring, Adjusting, and Moving On

Given the tall order that you had to help push your association's point of view, you have gotten your messaging down, determined whom you want to influence, developed a monitoring and early warning system, and executed on a variety of social media platforms, including websites, Facebook, Twitter, and others.

This is a fictitious exercise, so unfortunately, we don't get a report card at the end. In the real world as well, issue debates can drag on for years without one side really making "progress" on the issue—no report cards there, either. But during this, as in other types of online campaigns, you will constantly redo the basic steps, refining as you go along. You will:

- Continually test the effectiveness of your messaging;
- Adjust the content and frequency of your online advertising frequently, oftentimes on a daily basis;
- Continue to align your online strategy and tactics with what your colleagues are doing offline (earned media, grassroots, lobbying, etc.);

- Discover, develop, and deploy new tools as they become influential;

- Reach out to new influencers as they appear as well as work with your own allies, and

- At all times, measure what you set out to do against the results that you have achieved.

Summary

There is no "magic bullet" to make a troublesome reputational problem go away, especially in the case as I have described here. It can be *really hard* to convince people to alter their behavior or beliefs, especially when the option that they can employ is just avoiding your additive.

And just as there are no magic bullets, there are no magic formulas to ensure success online. During all of the phases of this campaign, being a good internal communicator is essential: tell your superiors and colleagues what you are doing, how well it's working, and if it is or it is not going well, tell them why—and what you will do in the future. Remember that you got hired because of your expertise, but you will still have to do a lot of teaching and evangelizing throughout what would likely be a long and drawn-out issue campaign.

In chapter 12, I'll sum up much of what we have covered in this book and talk about the question that is often asked of social media practitioners: "What's next?"

CHAPTER 12
SO, WHAT'S NEXT?

"The future is called 'perhaps,' which is the only possible
thing to call the future. And the only important
thing is not to allow that to scare you."
—Tennessee Williams, *Orpheus Descending, 1957*

This is the last chapter in the book. When I reach the end of a task, whether it's a work project, cleaning up after dinner, or running a road race, I usually ask myself "so, what's next?" I'm restless and find little time to savor one thing before I move on to the next, but that may well be one of the principal reasons that I have chosen a career in social media. The medium and the careers that comprise it are *about what's next.*

In this chapter, "what's next?" means two things: (a) what's next in the world of social media, and (b) what's next for you as you grow, advance, and truly blossom in your own career in social media.

The Ash Heap of Social Media History

In a 1982 speech to the British parliament, then President Ronald Reagan uttered the following prescient words about the fall of Communism: " [It is] the march of free- dom and democracy which will leave Marxism-Leninism on the ash heap of history as it has left other tyrannies which stifle the freedom and muzzle the self-expression of the people."[lxxxvii] The term "ash heap of history" has since found its way into our lexicon.

Social media has an ash heap of history made up of the smoldering embers of what was supposed to be the next "hot" thing, which "exploded" on to the social media scene, and then "flamed" out (please forgive all of the puns). If you want to get a sense of how the ninjas, gurus, and swamis can get their predictions wrong, think about how many social media sites you use regularly. Maybe it's YouTube, Facebook, Twitter, and perhaps now, Pinterest. Then compare this list to those properties that are on the ash heap of social media history.

In 2011, Simply Zesty put together a great list of "Nine Examples Of Social Media Sites That Failed Spectacularly."[lxxxviii] They list nine and I have excerpted the list and re-ordered the platforms beginning with those that I think are the most spectacular failures:

1. MySpace: At its most popular, the site had 75.9 million users in 2008. Yet the site's popularity began to decline as a lack of innovation and loyalty meant users flocked to Facebook instead. Numerous problems reared its head where spammers, viruses, porn, and even sexual predators had infiltrated the site and did very little to help MySpace's cause. The company was sold for $35 million this year, $525 million less than what News Corp bought it for back in 2005, making it a shadow of what it used to be. Launched: August 2003; finished: Still active.

2. Friendster: Friendster was a pioneer for social networks when it launched back in 2002, yet never fulfilled its potential. In its prime, the site had more than 115 million users in 2008, but a combination of shoddy programming, flawed infrastructure, and poor business decisions meant that the site went on a downward spiral. The collapse was so bad that the site is now the focus of

a Harvard Business School case study on how not to manage a tech company.[lxxxix] Launched: 2002; finished: May 2011 (rebranded).

3. Ping: Built into Apple's iTunes, Ping was advertised as a place where fans could connect with artists online; the huge factor behind its failure was that it never took into consideration that this was already being done on Twitter. Launched: September 2010; finished: Still active.

4. Yahoo! Buzz: Buzz borrowed a lot of its ideas from the website Digg and allowed users to vote for or against stories that they had read online. However, Yahoo's user base didn't care for the new addition and the fact that the platform was buggy. Launched: February 2008; finished: April 2011.

5. ConnectU: Formally HarvardConnection, the site formed by Mark Zuckerberg's Harvard classmates, Cameron and Tyler Winklevoss, was what Zuckerberg was supposed to help on before he decided to create Facebook instead. Launched: May 2004; finished: Currently inactive.

6. VitalSkate: one of three sites designed to unite skateboarders and extreme sport enthusiasts together. Launched: December 2006; finished: May 2008.

7. The Hub: Wal-Mart decided upon a new way to promote its back to school campaign by creating a social media site aimed solely at teenagers. Users would create profiles and be encouraged to upload photos and videos alongside shopping list of what Wal-Mart products they wanted most. It failed because very few people used the site.Launched:

July 2006; finished: September 2006 (ten weeks after it launched).

8. Orkut: Named after its creator, Orkut Büyükköten, Google's answer to social media failed to have any impact whatsoever and attracted controversy due to its lack of privacy and its use for criminal activity. Launched: January 2004; finished: Still active.

9. iYomu: Launched back in 2007, the New Zealand–based website aimed to be the social media site for 'grown-ups' around the world and aimed to have 10 million users by Christmas 2007. The site failed for numerous reasons, the main two being: first, Facebook already existed, which already catered to that demographic; second: joining meant having to fill out a lengthy questionnaire about yourself which many found tedious. Launched: August 2007; finished: June 2008.

What's Next in Social Media

In my career, I've been fortunate to have had many speaking engagements, and usually at some point in the question and answer sessions I'll get the question, "So, what's going to be the next big thing in social media?" My answer is invariably, "I have no idea whatsoever, and anyone who tells you that they know is a liar." Strong words, but I believe equally as strongly in them.

In a field in which the only constant is change, social media moves so rapidly that it is nearly impossible to predict what will become popular out of the thousands of new apps, platforms, and social networking tools that come out every year. My friend Chip Griffin, founder and CEO of eOutreach.com, sums it up succinctly:

"Effective communicators go where the audience is. We have enough to do without making difficult bets on what's next. Unless your target market is early adopters, you're better off focusing on the present than the future. Or as I like to say: if I knew what the 'next big thing' was, I'd be out building it. If you can see the future, head straight to Vegas and start laying down bets so you can take early retirement."[xc]

Who'd Have Thunk It?

When my friend Chuck DeFeo was the e-campaign manager for the Bush/Cheney 2004 campaign, Facebook was in a dorm in Harvard, YouTube did not yet exist, and the big social media property was Friendster. That's right, Friendster.

Considered the pioneer of social networking sites, Friendster was founded in 2002. Fast-forward a few years and Facebook (and for a while, MySpace) came along and demolished Friendster; it became an afterthought. By the way, Friendster is now "a social gaming site that is based in Kuala Lumpur, Malaysia."[xci] Friendster was first and it was King—for a day. And many said that it was the "next big thing." Yeah, it was—for about ten minutes.

Friendster Wasn't "The Next Big Thing"—Facebook and YouTube Were

Even with the appearance and disappearance of sites like Friendster and MySpace, almost no one could have predicted with any degree of credibility or accuracy the impact that Facebook or YouTube would have on our daily interactions. No one. I have mentioned Facebook many times in this book, and that is because it has evolved from a technology platform to a website that is woven into the global social fabric. As of December 2011, Facebook had[xcii]:

- 900 million monthly active users;
- 500 million daily active users;
- 425 million monthly active users who used Facebook mobile products; and
- [Pages in] more than 70 languages.

"Wow" Moment for Me, Version #1: Facebook

Even though I had been a Facebook user for some time, the first "oh, wow" moment for me was in September of 2009 when I traveled to Munich, Germany, for the two hundredth anniversary of Octoberfest. My friend Dave, who operates a tour company, put together a group of us for a four-day extravaganza that was filled with excellent food, interesting city sites, culture, and oh—ungodly amounts of German beer swilled in the beer tents in Munich. What does this mean for Facebook?

Our fun group of about twenty people was pretty diverse: some Americans, some Brits, some Germans, and a couple of people from other countries. As we became friendlier during our stay (and perhaps enhanced by copious amount of German beer), we all vowed to stay in touch. So rather than exchanging email addresses, one day while sitting in the lobby of our hotel, we all pulled out our smart-phones, and *without asking each other if we were on Facebook,* began sending each other friend requests. Facebook went from a "maybe" to a "given." Facebook crossed physical and linguistic barriers. No matter where we were from, we did not ask if the other was on Facebook, we assumed that we were—and were right. Within our group of twenty, and despite differences in our backgrounds, ages, and incomes, each and every single one of us was on Facebook. And many of us continue to stay in touch.

YouTube, Too

YouTube has gone from a video-sharing site to the world's second largest search engine. These statistics, compiled at the end of 2011, are telling:[xciii]

- 60 hours of video are uploaded every minute, or one hour of video is uploaded to YouTube every second;
- Over four billion videos are viewed a day;
- Over three billion hours of video are watched each month on YouTube;

- More video is uploaded to YouTube in one month than the three major U.S. networks created in sixty years; and

- In 2011, YouTube had more than one trillion views or almost 140 views for every person on earth.

"Wow" Moment for Me, Version #2: YouTube

Returning to my Octoberfest example, while in Munich, I was teasing one of my German friends about the Germans' supposed infatuation with David Hasselhoff (she was not amused, however, and asked me why Americans always ask that stupid question. Oops). I quickly changed the subject and asked her if she had seen the famous/infamous video of an extremely drunk David Hasselhoff attempting to eat a hamburger while lying on the floor. The video was taken by Hasselhoff's daughter in an attempt to get him to stop drinking.[xciv] *Even the non-English fluent members of our group,* when they heard the words "David Hasselhoff" and "hamburger," began mimicking eating a hamburger and staggering around drunk. As I write this, that video taken in 2010 has been viewed more than one million times. This example shows once again how social media—specifically, one very memorable YouTube video—had crossed language, time, and distance barriers. I sure hope that David Hasselhoff has gotten some help for his drinking, because that was one sad video.

So, Who Predicted This, Exactly?

Especially when it comes to social media, everyone likes predictions of what will be the "next big thing." Perhaps Mark Zuckerberg predicted that Facebook would go from a college website to a deeply embedded thread of the social fabric, but I cast a dubious eye towards those who say that they can predict the future of social media. Social media changes too fast, and when you combine this speed with the relative ease of market entry (cheap, affordable tools) and highly connected communities that can help spread the word, new social networking platforms come and go all the time.

What about Pinterest?

During the months that I have spent writing this book, the site Pinterest has begun drawing attention and millions of users. A November 22, 2011, article in *TechCrunch*, "Pinterest Is Now Pulling In More Pageviews Than Etsy; Grew 2,000% Since June," notes:

> *Online pinboard Pinterest is the new hotness. VCs [venture capitalists] are piling in because it is growing like crazy. How crazy? According to comScore, Pinterest generated 421 million pageviews in the U.S. in October, up 2,000 percent since June when it was at an estimated 20 million. Pinterest, which is still in an invite-only beta, has already surpassed the U.S. pageviews of much more established sites such as Etsy (which grew a healthy 47 percent since June to 348 million pageviews in October)."*[xcv]

By the time that this book is published, I have no idea if Pinterest will end up being a passing fancy like Friendster or a mainstay like Facebook (my prediction: passing fancy). My point is that even when an online property comes on to the scene out of nowhere, one cannot predict its staying power.

I look at predictions about social media like weather forecasts: people pay close attention when it's important to them ("Is it going to rain on my wedding day tomorrow?"), but quickly forget the prediction when time has passed. I could fill up the remaining pages of this book with failed social media predictions, but if no one remembers what the weatherman said on TV after the day has passed, why focus on that?

How You Can Have a Sense of What's the Next Big Thing[xcvi]

I don't know anyone who has a functioning crystal ball and who can accurately predict the future, let alone which social media properties will be the winners, and which will end up on the "ash heap of history." As a top-notch social media practitioner, it is your job to *know about what is hot* and continually analyze it to see if its use makes business sense for your employer or your clients. That means trying out everything: Quora, Google+, Pinterest, and others. Some may be useful for a while (MySpace), some may bomb right out of the gate (The Hub), and others may hold people's attention simply because of who backs it (Ping). To be a successful social media practitioner, you need to stay up-to-date on what these platforms can do, and more importantly, what they can do for you.

Knowing Who to Believe: Avoiding Snake Oil Salesmen

Many people claim to know what the next big thing will be, or the next "game-changing" platform. (I automatically distrust anyone who uses the term "game-changing," because I think it's so shallow, overused, and essentially meaningless). When you are starting and advancing your career, to stay smart, you'll have to consume a lot of information, but need a "B.S. detector," one that will help you separate good, actionable advice offered by smart people from pedestrian clichés served up as groundbreaking news.

In the field of social media, those who are highly recognized as experts are called "A-listers" (ironically, like comedians) or "cewebrities." Many of their blogs are widely read, their opinions sought, and ironically (from my point of view since you are reading this book), they write books. Lots of books.

One of the hardest things to do when you are seeking knowledge and looking to pick up valuable insights is deciding whose opinion to follow. I'll not name names here because it's not fair, but there are wildly successful social media "gurus" (I despise this term) who spout advice, tent their fingers, and speak in platitudes. They have thousands of followers on Twitter, have widely read books, and are quoted extensively. Does this make them experts, worthy of your following them and learning from them? Maybe, and maybe not.

I owe the inspiration on many of the topics in this book to a "secret group" on Facebook that I belong to made up of about seventy-five people who I think are among the thought leaders in the field. They not only come up with original ideas, but they are experts in calling out those who are, well, phoneys. Snake oil salesmen. Those who get paid to offer advice that is a dressed-up firm grasp of the obvious. As a group, it drives us crazy, because these so-called experts pollute the space and make it harder for those of us who try to be practical social media practitioners to offer points of view that counter those of the "ninjas and gurus." I have heard from more than one client that [this ninja] "has written a book and was a keynote speaker at BlogWorld Expo and says the opposite, so why should I believe you?" It's frustrating because it's not about who is smarter, it's about who offers the most *practical advice*. Advice that works for a mom-and-pop organization as well as a Fortune 500 company because it is grounded and practical, not "game-changing."

Whom to Trust?

There are a few ways that you can help separate the wheat from the chaff, the "gurus" from those who offer practical, actionable advice and opinions that can help make you a smarter social media person.

Some solid advice comes from Brian Carter, whose book *The Like Economy* offers some simple advice on whom to trust with your valuable time and attention. He boils down his thinking into two simple and elegant questions:

1. What specific, measurable results has this expert helped companies achieve?
2. What types of businesses has he worked with?

In short, although some of the aforementioned "gurus" can write books, give speeches, tent their fingers, and speak of "game-changers," what have they *actually accomplished* for clients? What are the industries that they have helped to achieve measurable results? In short, you need to try to determine if they can actually walk the walk in addition to talking the talk.

Another interviewee for this book (whose name I will leave out, not because he has asked me too, but because of the nature of his remarks) offers a similarly stark point of view regarding snake oil salesmen. His take? "The definition [of social media phoneys] is people doing something for their own financial gain that they know is not true! I think these guys are smart enough to know that is B.S. and what they are saying is not true. Many of them are not just frauds, they are liars who have gotten rich off of it."

More good ninja-spotting advice comes from Christopher Barger, author of the *Social Media Strategist* and the former head of social media for General Motors. He sums up his feelings succinctly in his book, but importantly, from the perspective of a potential employer[xcvii]: "In some circles in the social media world, it's become vogue to refer to one's self as a social media 'ninja,' 'Jedi,' or 'guru.' Supposedly, this is meant to convey not only levels of expertise and skill that exceed that of the average professional, but also a superior grade of hipsterism and nonconformity. In reality, these self-granted titles scream immaturity and don't have anything to do with the job you are hiring for. (Unless you are really looking for an actual assassin or intergalactic quasi-religious warrior, that is—in which case, the winning candidate likely won't leave business cards). Calling one's self a ninja, Jedi, guru, rock star, etc. reveals the candidate to be far more concerned with image than results, style over substance. No one who wishes to be taken seriously as a professional should use the same business title as a bunch of cartoon turtles with a fondness for pizza. And any business that wants its social media leader—and by extension its social media program—taken seriously both internally and externally will reject this kind of silliness."

Sniffing Out the Snake Oil Salesmen—Look for Clues

To make yourself smarter as you work to study up on social media, when you are reading blogs, books, or magazine articles, like a detective, look for clues. Has this person *accomplished something in the social media space aside from giving advice?* Do her books offer case-study advice based upon campaigns that she has designed, executed, and implemented? Is the success measurable? And if so, has she won any awards that recognize a particular accomplishment, like a Webby? Look for people who are working with clients (or have) on a daily basis as opposed to those who support themselves through speaking engagements ginned up by a large number of Twitter followers.

Advancing Your Career by Being a Good Communicator

We have covered a lot of ground in this book about the importance of developing good communications skills, but enhancing your ability to communicate effectively at work doesn't stop once you get hired. Like many other skills, as your career moves forward, your skills should improve.

David Almacy, former Internet director in the White House, told me his view on what makes a good social media practitioner: "The quality is that they have to be good communicators, not just professionally, but personally as well. You have to be able to strategically think about not *what* messages resonate, but *how* they resonate. You need to think three moves ahead."

David's point is at the heart of what will bring you continued success in your career in social media. As a practitioner of social media, I don't and have never viewed myself as a technologist; I am a communicator. I take my employer or clients' words and messages and push them out to internal or external audiences.

Often times, in order to even gain consensus on launching an externally facing project, I first need to explain, teach, and evangelize for the use of a social media tool: communication. Within my current job at the Securities and Exchange Commission, I am surrounded by lawyers and accountants. I could not have had any success as new media director without the ability to think strategically about what will resonate with a naturally cautious securities lawyer to address her concerns about launching a new social media program: more communication. In short, I need to teach and sell internally before I do anything externally. Being a good communicator usually starts with influencing your colleagues before you can attempt to influence external stakeholders.

Stay Curious

Even when you have landed in a job and have a degree of success in social media, think about your job like that of a baseball player. You may have made it up through the minor leagues to the major leagues and have had some success. But as you move forward, there will a natural progression where a younger generation emerges who are preparing to play alongside you—and may "outplay" you. The field of social media is growing, as is its adoption as a business tool, so the way that you can "outplay" others is to learn, learn, and learn—keep yourself on top of (a) what is happening in the world of social media and (b) what some thought leaders (and not snake oil salesmen) think of the trends. This will help you form your own opinions and stay smart and sharp.

Top Five Suggested Sources

I have included a much larger suggested reading list in the appendix of this book, but based upon conversations with social media colleagues as well as with people whom I have interviewed for this book, I came up with a list of the five must-have sources to understand and stay on top of social media.

1. Mashable (mashable.com). This was the number one consensus read among those whom I interviewed for this book. "The web-site's primary focus is social media news, but also covers news

and developments in mobile, entertainment, online video, business, web development, technology, memes, and gadgets. With a reported 50+ million monthly page views, Mashable ranks as one of the world's largest websites."[xcviii]

2. TechCrunch (techcrunch.com). TechCrunch is more technology focused, but with a strong social media bent, and is ... "a leading technology media property, dedicated to obsessively profiling startups, reviewing new Internet products, and breaking tech news. Founded in June 2005, TechCrunch and its network of websites now reach over 12 million unique visitors and draw more than 37 million page views per month."[xcix]

3. *Fast Company* (fastcompany.com) is unique on this list because it offers both online and print versions. It combines articles about technology and social media with a focus on business. *Fast Company* provides "a unique editorial focus on innovation in technology, ethonomics (ethical economics), leadership, and design. Written for, by, and about the most progressive business leaders, *Fast Company* and FastCompany.com inspire readers and users to think beyond traditional boundaries, lead conversations, and create the future of business."[c]

4. Ragan Communications produces, among other publications, *Ragan's PR Daily* (prdaily.com/Main/AboutUs.aspx) and focuses on communications, public relations, and social media. It's a good addition to your reading list if you strive to stay on top of what is happening in communications as well as in technology and social media.[ci]

5. *For Immediate Release: The Hobson and Holtz Report* podcast (forimmediaterelease.biz). (Disclaimer: I have been a contributor and a cohost of this podcast, but I would not include it on this list if it did not offer tremendous value). Begun by Neville Hobson and Shel Holtz more than six hundred episodes ago, they modestly describe their show as "the weekly podcast of Neville Hobson, ABC, and Shel Holtz, ABC, a pair of

communication professionals who think they have something to say."[cii] First, I have recommended this because it is a *podcast*. You can listen to it while you are at the gym, driving, or any other quiet time you have. Second, no matter what the topic, show or opinions offered, for more than five years, I have always finished an episode having learned something new. Always. The podcast is entertaining, informative, and a must-have for the social media and communications pro.

Your Future

As I have noted several times just in this chapter, no one can predict the future. You, however, *control* your future in social media. Hopefully after reading this book, you feel a desire to learn more about, or else begin or enhance your career in social media.

I am a checklist sort of person, so summing up this book, if you want to move forward from a job to a career, read and eventually check off the items on this list. It's my suggested Road to Social Media Success:

- Decide if this is the path for you.
- Know that you have to start somewhere. It may be self-study, class work in a formal classroom setting, an internship, or all three.
- Be a practitioner. As you are learning about the tools like Facebook, Twitter, blogs, or Pinterest, use them. And put the "social" in "social media" by interacting with other people.
- Learn to be a good, versatile writer.
- Use social media tools like LinkedIn to advertise yourself, then use the same tools like Facebook to actively seek out job openings.
- Be active in your job search. Seek out employers and cities that are attractive to you. Don't just wait to be contacted.

- As you learn about the field and employers, try to make sense of job titles. They indicate what you can do to prepare yourself to work in the field, as well as what you may end up doing.

- Make use of all of the offline resources you can, like good, old-fashioned networking, and temporary and permanent recruitment firms.

- When you get an interview, use your social media research skills to prepare you by knowing something about the people with whom you will interview, the job offered, and the company.

- When you get hired, understand that this is the beginning, not the end of being a good communicator. Remember that your job will be to influence people throughout your career.

- To advance your career in social media, map out your goals and choose work that fits those goals. And understand that your job will consist of making people happy.

- Stay on top of the strategies, tools, and tactics that are helping your peers be successful, and avoid snake oil salesmen.

- Understand that you career in social media, if you are twenty-two or sixty-two, will be to "figure it out."

Summary: What's Next for You

Do you ever get one of those ridiculous financial statements from your 401(k) or some other legal form that has ten bazillion pages of unintelligible information followed by one blank piece of paper that says that the page has been left blank—intentionally? I have left the preceding portion blank because, by this point, you have most likely learned that there are many different directions that you can take in preparing yourself for a career in social media, choosing the job that will interest you most, and navigating staying on top of what is new to continually communicate to both internal and external audiences what you think will help them have a successful social media program.

It's All about You

It's all up to you, however. YOU will fill in the blank page. To prepare yourself for a career in social media, you can choose one of the growing numbers of university-level programs like Auburn University or the University of Maryland University College to get classroom study. You can parlay an undergraduate degree (or one in progress) in communications or technology into an internship, which is a great way to take a career for a test drive. You can become self-taught through sheer drive and determination, like Antonia Harler, whom we met in earlier chapters. You can start as a rocket engineer like Evan Kraus, transition to online, and "figure it out." You can learn HTML from a book like Chuck DeFeo, and land yourself or your boss in the *New York Times* simply by raising your hand and volunteering to do something that has never been done.

Or you could be like this author and start out in a completely different career at an abysmal salary and not really figure out what you want to be in social media when you grow up until you figure it out. We all have taken different paths to get where we are.

The bottom line is, with some intellectual curiosity, hard work, good planning, lots of reading, writing practice, and actually performing social media tasks, you too can start that career in social media—and become a smashing success.

You can do it.

I hope that you have enjoyed reading this book as much as I have writing it. I love keeping in touch with people, so please feel free to drop me an email and let me know how *you* are doing in your career in social media: mark@startingacareerinsocialmedia.com.

Mark Story
Washington, DC

APPENDIX
SUGGESTED READING LIST

Throughout the process of writing this book, I spoke with many people and always asked them what they read for information to stay current in their own social media careers. The list below (most of which you could pull into an RSS reader and make into your go-to list, by the way) is compiled from my own reading and listening lists along with what some of the best social media practitioners recommend. I could write a whole different book and what to read and why, so I have kept this list short and concise.

Online News and Commentary

- Fast Company: http://www.fastcompany.com. Also a print magazine, Fast Company offers "a unique editorial focus on innovation in technology, ethonomics (ethical economics), leadership, and design. Written for, by, and about the most progressive business leaders, *Fast Company* and FastCompany.com inspire readers and users to think beyond traditional boundaries, lead conversations, and create the future of business."

- Mashable: http://mashable.com. "Mashable's mission is to empower and inspire people by spreading knowledge of social media and technology." This was the virtually unanimous choice of a "must-read" by those whom I interviewed for the book.

- The Next Web, http://thenextweb.com. "Founded in 2008, The Next Web is one of the world's largest online publications that delivers an international perspective on the latest news about Internet technology, business and culture. With an active, influential audience consisting of more than 5.1 million monthly visits and over 7 million monthly page views."

- Read/Write/Web, www.readwriteweb.com. "ReadWriteWeb is one of the most popular technology blogs in the world, known for offering insightful analysis about each day's Internet industry news."

- Tech Crunch: www.techcrunch.com, a group-edited website about technology start-ups, particularly the Web 2.0 sector. This site was the second choice of those interviewed for the book, behind Mashable, as a "must-read" resource.

Blogs

- The All Blogs: www.AllTwitter.com, www.AllFacebook.com. Both are topic-specific and provide information that is only about Facebook or only about Twitter. If you want to stay up-to-date on these two social media tools, this is the place to get your information.

- David Armano's *Logic+Emotion* blog, darmano.typepad.com. Now a senior executive at Edelman's digital practice, David's blog often presents information that is boiled down to infographics, making it easier to distill and understand complex social media topics.

- Danny Brown's blog: dannybrown.me, *The Human Side of Media and the Social Side of Marketing*. Danny is smart, sarcastic and Scottish.

- Jason Falls's *Social Media Explorer*, www.socialmediaexplorer. com. This blog provides excellent perspective on the current state of social media and should be a regular stop for serious social media marketers. Jason also provides a touch of snark, which I love.

- Robert French's PR Open Mic: www.propenmic.org. I mentioned it in Chapter 2, but it's an online resource that connects students, faculty, and social media and public relations practitioners, offering biography pages (an online resume of sorts), member-based blogs, discussion forums, video interviews with prominent practitioners, networking events and opportunities for extended learning, job boards, and what I think is most important, a place for people (mainly students) to post their own resumes. It is a groundbreaking, helpful and a terrific resource if you are thinking about starting a career in social media.

- Maddie Grant's *Social Fish* blog: www.socialfish.org. Maddie is one of the coauthors of the book *Humanize* along with one of the owners of the consultancy Social Fish, based in Washington, DC. They do most of their work for associations and nonprofits and this blog is a great read if you are considering a social media career in these fields.

- Neville Hobson's blog: www.nevillehobson.com. Neville is a communicator, blogger, and podcaster, one of the leading European early adopters, opinion-leaders, and influencers in digital communication for business. One half of the do-not-miss podcast, *For Immediate Release: The Hobson and Holtz Report*, reading what Neville has to say will give you a European- and technology-focused view of social media.

- Shel Holtz's blog, holtz.com/blog. I could recite a lot of exemplary items about Shel like the fact that he is a five-time winner of IABC's Gold Quill award and was named IABC/Los Angeles's Communicator of the Year, but that still does not do him justice. In my mind, he is the godfather of online public relations and is someone through his books, speeches, interviews, and most importantly his *For Immediate Release* podcast with Neville Hobson, will just make you smarter.

- Kami Huyse's *Communications Overtones*, overtonecomm. blogspot.com. Kami is "a seventeen-year-veteran of public relations, she speaks at social media events and conferences all over the country, and her work in social media has earned her the SNCR's 2008 and 2010 awards and IABC's 2009 Gold Quill of Excellence Award. She ran the virtual PR agency, My PR Pro, from 2002–2009 and is the strategic architect for many successful social media campaigns."

- Mitch Joel's *Six Pixels of Separation*, www.twistimage.com/blog. *Marketing Magazine* dubbed him the "Rock Star of Digital Marketing" and called him, "one of North America's leading digital visionaries."

- Shelly Kramer's *V3 Integrated Marketing Blog*, www.v3im.com/ blog. All social media, all the time, and smart commentary.

- Katie Payne's *PR Measurement Blog*, kdpaine.blogs.com. This blog is self-described as follows: "If you've ever wondered how to measure social media, public relations, public affairs, media relations, internal communications, or blogs, you're in the right spot. In this space I'll be regularly ranting and raving about news, techniques, and development in the world of PR research and evaluation."

- Public Relations Matters, www.publicrelationsmatters.com. Barbara Nixon has a PhD and teaches at Southeastern University and her blog deals with "public relations and public communication. Most of the posts are geared toward my students." But here's the cool part: by reading what she has to say, it's almost like being part of her class. You can read her thinking and keep up with what is going on in her classes. Along with Robert French, Barbara is one of the true pioneers of teaching at the intersection of public relations and social media.

- The Social Media Informer, www.socialmediainformer.com. A new website which brings together advice and insights from an all-star team of social media bloggers.

- Spin Sucks, www.spinsucks.com, by Gini Dietrich. Her own description: "Gini Dietrich, is the lead author . . . you never really know what you're going to get, but you can bet when she's upset about something, she'll rally the lovers and the haters for one common cause (unless it's about wearing jeans to speak—then there is no rallying)."

Books

- *The Cluetrain Manifesto*, www.cluetrain.com. Written in 1999, it is widely recognized as one of the best books about what was then not yet called "social media." Out of publication now, but available electronically.

- Charlene Li's *Groundswell: Winning in a World Transformed by Social Technologies*, coauthored by Josh Bernoff, published in 2009.

The book is self-described as: "When consumers you've never met are rating your company's products in public forums with which you have no experience or influence, your company is vulnerable. In *Groundswell*, Charlene Li and Josh Bernoff of Forrester, Inc. explain how to turn this threat into an opportunity."

- *Measuring Public Relationships: The Data-Driven Communicator's Guide to Success*, Katie Delahaye Paine, KDPaine & Partners, LLC, December 12, 2007. If you want to understand why measurement is critical to an effective public relations campaign—and how to do it—buy this book.

- *The Social Media Bible*, by David K. Brake and Lon Safko. www. thesocialmediabible.com. I used this as a textbook in my classes at the University of Maryland University College. It is a LONG book—nearly eight hundred pages—but is full of practical information and "tactics, tools, and strategies for business success."

NOTES

i.   IMDB page on "Office Space", accessed April 1, 2012: http://www.imdb.com/title/tt0151804/

ii.   Jenise Uehara Henrickson, "The Growth of Social Media: An Infographic," The Search Engine Journal (2011): accessed November 30, 2011, http://www.searchenginejournal.com/the-growth-of-social-media-an-infographic/32788/.

iii.   Facebook Fact Sheet, Facebook Newsroom, accessed March 19, 2012: http://newsroom.fb.com/content/default.aspx?NewsAreaId=22.

iv.   Mariel Loveland, "How Social Media Has Grown Over the Years," Scribbal.com (2011): accessed March 27, 2012, www.scribbal.com/2011/08/infographic-how-social-media-has-grown-over-the-years/.

v.   Accessed from Jess3, an "Internet visualization" company located in Washington, DC: www.jess3.com/

vi.   Joanna Brenner, "Pew Internet: Mobile," Pew Internet and American Life Project (2012): accessed December 3, 2011, www.pewinternet.org/Commentary/2012/February/Pew-Internet-Mobile.aspx.

vii.   "Myspace, Facebook, Linkedin, Social Networking Job Trends," SimplyHired.com (2012): accessed January 2012, www.simplyhired.com/a/jobtrends/trend/q-MySpace percent2C+Facebook percent2C+LinkedIn percent2C+percent22Social+Networking percent22

viii.   Julia Angwin, Shayndi Raice and Spencer E. Ante, "Facebook Retreats on Privacy," Wall Street Journal

(2011): accessed January 29, 2012, http://online. wsj.com/video/facebook-retreats-in-privacy-issue/11FEC5E6-90BA-40C5-A1A4-4BCC0EB19D48. html

ix.   Interview with David Almacy conducted via Skype, January 20, 2012.

x.   Interview with Dr. Julia Hill, conducted via Skype, March 28, 2012.

xi.   Interview with Robert French conducted via Skype, December 28, 2011.

xii.   Marta Antelo, "Internships Have Value, Whether or Not Students Are Paid," Chronicle of Higher Education (2011): accessed February 2, 2012, http://chronicle.com/article/Internships-Have-Value/127231/.

xiii.   Interview with David Almacy, conducted via Skype, January 20, 2012.

xiv.   Interview with Dr. Julia Hill, conducted via Skype, March 28, 2012.

xv.   Christopher Witt, Real Leaders Don't Do PowerPoint: How to Sell Yourself and Your Ideas (New York: Crown Business) 2009.

xvi.   Amy Gallo, "Boost Your Career with Social Media: Tips for the Uninitiated," *Harvard Business Review* Blogs (2011): accessed February 3, 2012, http:// blogs.hbr.org/hmu/2011/12/boost-your-career-with-social.html

xvii.   Jeff Weiner, ""100 million members and counting...", LinkedIn Blog, (2011): accessed March 6, 2012, http://blog.linkedin.com/2011/03/22/linkedin-100-million/

xviii.   Email interview with Mike DelPonte, December 28, 2011.

xix.   Linda Coles, "10 Tips for Finding a Job Using Facebook and LinkedIn," Social Media Examiner, (2010): accessed March 4, 2012, www. socialmediaexaminer.com/10-tips-for-finding-a-job-using-facebook-and-linkedin/.

xx.   Justin McMurdo, "My Awesome Video Resume," accessed March 12, 2012 http://www.youtube.com/ watch?v=2MRE7rjLocc

xxi.   The Resume Bear, "How many people are using YouTube to post video resumes?" The Resume Bear, (2011): accessed March 12, 2012, http:// blog.resumebear.com/uncategorized/how-many-people-are-using-youtube-to-post-video-resumes/

xxii.   Interview with Evan Kraus conducted via Skype, December 22, 2011.

xxiii.   Interview with Robert French conducted via Skype, December 28, 2011.

xxiv.   Diane Coutu, Jeffrey A. Joerres, Michael Fertik, John G. Palfrey Jr., Danah M. Boyd, "We Googled You," *Harvard Business Review*: (2007). Accessed February 3, 3012, http://hbr.org/product/we-googled-you-harvard-business-review/an/R0706A-PDF-ENG

xxv.   *ibid*

xxvi.   Interview with Antonia Harler conducted via Skype, December 4, 2011.

xxvii.   *ibid*

xxviii.   Megan O'Neill, "36.6 Million Americans Got Their Current Jobs Through Social Media [Infographic]," (2011): Accessed February 22, 2012, http:// socialtimes.com/36-6-million-americans-got-their-current-jobs-through-social-media-infographic_ b86495

xxix.   Interview with David Almacy conducted via Skype, January 20, 2012.

xxx.   Interview with Chuck DeFeo conducted via Skype, March 12, 2012.

xxxi.   Interview with Antonia Harler conducted via Skype, December 4, 2011.

xxxii.   Interview with Evan Kraus conducted via Skype, December 22, 2011.

xxxiii.   Steve Toth, "Baidu Makes Gains and Google Pays the Price," TechWyse, (2012): accessed April 2, 2012, http://www.techwyse.com/blog/internet-marketing/search-engine-market-share-for-february-2012/.

xxxiv.   "Alexander J.A.M. van Deursen, Jan A.G.M. van Dijk, "Using the Internet: Skill related problems in users' online behavior," Department of Media, Communication and Organization, University of Twente, 7500 AE Enschede, The Netherlands (2008): accessed February 21, 2012, http://www.utwente.nl/gw/mco/bestanden/Using%20the%20Internet-%20Skill%20related%20problems.pdf.

xxxv.   Jacob Stoops, "Click Distribution & Percentages by SERP Rank," AgentSEO (2010): accessed February 26, 2012, http://www.agent-seo.com/seo/click-distribution-percentages-by-serp-rank/.

xxxvi.   Richard Nelson Bolles, What Color Is Your Parachute? A Practical Manual for Job-Hunters and Career-Changers. (New York: Ten Speed Press, 2009), Kindle edition.

xxxvii.   Sherri Dalphonse, Mary Clare Glover, Marisa M. Kashino, James Michael Causey, "50 Great Places to Work in Washington," Washingtonian Magazine (2011): accessed February 10, 2012, http://www.

washingtonian.com/articles/work-education/50-great-places-to-work-in-washington/.

xxxviii.   "Best Places to Work 2011," Crain's Business New York (2011): accessed February 10, 2012, www.crainsnewyork.com/gallery/20111204/FEATURES/113009999

xxxix.   100 best companies to work for," CNN Money (2011): accessed February 10, 2012, www.money.cnn.com/magazines/fortune/bestcompanies/2011/full_list/

xl.   Accessed from the Holmes Report website, February 22, 2012.

xli.   "Holmes Report Agency Directory" (2012), accessed February 22, 2012, www.holmesreport.com/research/agency-directory.aspx

xlii.   Kristin Piombino, "The ultimate guide to social media jobs and salaries," Ragan.com, (2012): accessed February 13, 2012, http://www.ragan.com/Main/Articles/44387.aspx.

xliii.   Megan O'Neill, "36.6 Million Americans Got Their Current Jobs Through Social Media [Infographic]," Social Times, (2011): accessed February 18, 2012, http://socialtimes.com/36-6-million-americans-got-their-current-jobs-through-social-media-infographic_b86495

xliv.   Heather R. Huhman, "Job Searching On Facebook: There Are Many Apps For That," Business Insider (2011): accessed February 13, 2012, http://www.businessinsider.com/job-searching-on-facebook-there-are-many-apps-for-that-2011-7#ixzz1iJha9Qun

xlv.   Lon Sakfo and David K. Brake, The Social Media Bible: Tactics, Tools and Strategies for Business

Success. (Hoboken, New Jersey: John Wiley and Sons, 2009).

xlvi.   Jennifer Mattern, "You're a Social Media Whatsit?—An Overabundance of Social Media Job Titles," social implications blog, (2011): accessed January 6, 2012, socialimplications.com/youre-a-social-media-whatsit-an-overabundance-of-social-media-job-titles/

xlvii.   *ibid.*

xlviii.   Katie Delahaye Paine, Measuring Public Relationships: The Data-Driven Communicator's Guide to Success, (New Hampshire: KDPaine & Partners, LLC, 2007).

xlix.   Michael Scissons, "A CEO's Guide To Social Media In 2012," Fast Company, (2011): accessed January 7, 2012, www.fastcompany.com/1800924/a-ceo-s-guide-to-social-media-in-2012.

l.   Mark Story, "Social Media: Things to Think About in Working for an Agency," (2012): accessed January 20, 2012, www.startingacareerinsocialmedia.com/2012/01/09/social-media-things-to-think-about-in-working-for-an-agency.

li.   Jakob Nielsen, "How Users Read on the Web," Jakob Nielsen's Alertbox (1997), accessed January 7, 2012, http://www.useit.com/alertbox/9710a.html.

lii.   Jason Falls, "The Ethics, or Lack Thereof, of Ghost Blogging," Social Media Explorer, (2009): accessed January 6, 2012, www.socialmediaexplorer.com/social-media-marketing/the-ethics-of-ghost-blogging/.

liii.   Brian Carter, "15 Facts About Social Media Every B2B Marketer Should Know," (2011): accessed January 20, 2012, www.briancarteryeah.com/blog/

facebook/15-facts-about-social-media-every-b2b-marketer-should-know/

liv.   Michelle Rafter, "Top 10 Tips for Finding Temp Work and Contract Gigs," The Second Act Blog, (2010): accessed January 16, 2012, www.secondact.com/2010/08/top-10-tips-for-finding-temp-work/

lv.   Jobs@NIH, National Institutes of Health, (2012), accessed January 27, 2012, www.jobs.nih.gov/jobsearch/qualsandksas.htm

lvi.   Skype interview with Evan Kraus, December 22, 2011.

lvii.   Christopher Barger, The Social Media Strategist: Build a Successful Career from the Inside Out. (New York: McGraw Hill. 2012), chapter 5: Deal Breakers.

lviii.   Jesse Thorn, "What podcasts do you subscribe to, Jesse?" (2012): accessed January 16, 2012, www.jessethorn.tumblr.com/post/15678234125/what-podcasts-do-you-subscribe-to-jesse-folks.

lix.   Mark Story, Job Seekers: Q&A With Brian Batchelder, Recruiter For Fleishman-Hillard, (2010). Accessed February 9, 2012,

lx.   http://www.intersectionofonlineandoffline.com/job-seekers-qa-with-brian-batcheler-recruiter-for-fleishman-hillard/

lxi.   Lon Sakfo and David K. Brake, The Social Media Bible: Tactics, Tools and Strategies for Business Success. (Hoboken, New Jersey: John Wiley and Sons, 2009).

lxii.   "Top U.S. Online Video Content Properties Ranked by Unique Video Viewers," comScore, (2011): accessed January 24, 2012, http://www.comscore.com/Press_Events/Press_Releases/2012/3/comScore_Releases_February_2012_U.S._Online_Video_Rankings

lxiii. Mark Story, "Social Media: being a user doesn't mean you are a good practitioner," AGBeat.com, (2012), accessed March 5, 2012, http://agbeat. com/real-estate-technology-new-media/social-media-being-a-user-doesnt-mean-you-are-a-good-practitioner/

lxiv. John P. Kotter and James L. Haskett, Corporate Culture, (New York: Simon and Schuster, Inc., 1992).

lxv. Interview with Christopher Barger conducted via Skype, April 6, 2012.

lxvi. ibid.

lxvii. Small Business Administration, "Summary of Size Standards by Industry, Services Industry," (2012): accessed February 11, 2012, http://www.sba.gov/content/summary-size-standards-industry.

lxviii. Interview with Kristen D. Wesley conducted via Skype, April 5, 2012.

lxix. "Historical trends in the usage of traffic analysis tools for websites," W3 Techs, accessed February 10, 2012, http://w3techs.com/technologies/history_overview/traffic_analysis/all.

lxx. Interview with David Almacy conducted via Skype, January 20, 2012.

lxxi. Interview with Geoff Livingston, conducted via Skype, March 30, 2012.

lxxii. Interview with Christopher Barger, conducted via Skype, April 6, 2012.

lxxiii. Mark Story, "Social Media Survival, What to Do When You are Running Into a Managerial or Client Brick Wall," Intersection of Online and Offline, (2011), accessed February 11, 2012, www.intersectionofonlineandoffline.com/social-media-survival-what-to-do-when-you-are-running-into-managerial-or-client-brick-wall/.

lxxiv.   Edelman Trust Barometer, (2012): accessed February 19, 2012, www.trust.edelman.com.

lxxv.   The Edelman Trust Barometer, "About Trust" (2012): accessed February 19, 2012, www.trust.edelman.com/about-trust/.

lxxvi.   *ibid.*

lxxvii.   *ibid.*

lxxviii.   "Mom Bloggers' Voices and Votes Influence State of the Union," Scarborough Research, (2011): accessed February 21, 2012, http://www.scarborough.com/press-release.php?press_id=mom-bloggers-voices-and-votes-influence-state-of-the-union.

lxxix.   Allison Aubrey, "McDonald's Courts Mom Bloggers When Changing The Menu," National Public Radio, (2011): accessed February 20, 2012, http://www.npr.org/blogs/health/2011/07/27/138746335/mcdonalds-courts-mom-bloggers-when-changing-the-menu.

lxxx.   Marti Barletta, "Marketing to Women Quick Facts," SheConomy.com, (2012). Accessed April 4, 2012, http://www.she-conomy.com/facts-on-women.

lxxxi.   Email interview with Brian Carter, February 24, 2012.

lxxxii.   "Directory of Companies in Social Media Analysis," Social Media Analysis Blog, accessed February 24, 2012,

lxxxiii.   www.socialmediaanalysis.com/directory/.

lxxxiv.   Lisa Barone, "5 Reasons NOT to Delete Negative Reviews," Outspoken Media, (2010): accessed February 19, 2012, http://outspokenmedia.com/reputation-management/5-reasons-not-to-delete-negative-reviews/.

lxxxv.   Marc Gunther, "Corporate blogging: Wal-Mart's fumbles," CNN Money, (2006): accessed February 15, 2012, http://money.cnn.com/2006/10/17/technology/pluggedin_gunther_blog.fortune/index.htm

lxxxvi.   "How to Pitch SME," Social Media Explorer, accessed February 20, 2012, www.socialmediaexplorer.com.

lxxxvii.   The History Place, Great Speeches Collection, Ronald Reagan Address to the British Parliament, accessed April 4, 2012, http://www.historyplace.com/speeches/reagan-parliament.htm.

lxxxviii.   "Nine Examples Of Social Media Sites That Failed Spectacularly," Simply Zesty, (2011): accessed on March 23, 2012,

lxxxix.   http://www.simplyzesty.com/social-media/nine-examples-of-social-media-sites-that-failed-spectacularly/

xc.   Mikolaj Jan Piskorski, Carin-Isabel Knoop, "Friendster (A)," Harvard Business Review, (2006): accessed April 4, 2012, http://hbr.org/product/friendster-a/an/707409-PDF-ENG.

xci.   Email interview with Chip Griffin, March 27, 2012.

xcii.   Friendster Wikipedia entry, accessed on March 19, 2012, http://en.wikipedia.org/wiki/Friendster.

xciii.   Facebook Fact Sheet, Facebook Newsroom, accessed March 19, 2012:

xciv.   http://newsroom.fb.com/content/default.aspx?NewsAreaId=22

xcv.   YouTube Statistics, accessed on March 19, 2012, http://www.youtube.com/t/press_statistics

xcvi.   "David Hasselhoff grateful daughter taped him eating hamburger drunk," The Daily Telegraph (Australia), (2010): accessed March 13, 2012,

| | http://www.dailytelegraph.com.au/lifestyle/diet-fitness/david-hasselhoff-grateful-daughter-taped-him-eating-hamburger-drunk/story-e6frf019-1225966477579 |

xcvii.   Erick Schonfeld, "Pinterest Is Now Pulling In More Pageviews Than Etsy; Grew 2,000% Since June" TechCrunch, (2011): accessed March 24, 2012, http://techcrunch.com/2011/11/22/pinterest-pageviews-etsy-grew-2000/

xcviii. Christopher Barger, The Social Media Strategist: Build a Successful Career from the Inside Out. (New York: McGraw Hill. 2012), chapter 5: Deal Breakers.

xcix.   Mashable, retrieved from Wikipedia on March 24, 2012, http://en.wikipedia.org/wiki/Mashable

c.   TechCrunch, retrieved from "About TechCrunch" on March 24, 2012, http://techcrunch.com/about/.

ci.   Fast Company About Us, retrieved on March 24, 2012, http://www.fastcompany.com/about-us.

cii.   About Ragan's PR Daily, accessed on April 4, 2012 www.prdaily.com/Main/AboutUs.aspx.

ciii.   About FIR, accessed on March 24, 2012, http://www.forimmediaterelease.biz/index.php?/weblog/about_us/

INDEX